THE GUINNESS BOOK OF
1953

Kenneth Macksey

GUINNESS SUPERLATIVES LIMITED
2 CECIL COURT, LONDON ROAD, ENFIELD, MIDDLESEX

ACKNOWLEDGEMENTS

Photographs supplied by **POPPERFOTO**
Additional photographs:

Aluminium Company of Canada, Ltd: p 66 (bottom);
Associated Newspapers Group Ltd: p 6 (top centre,
bottom right, p 7 (top left);
Beaverbrook Newspapers Ltd: p 6 (top and
bottom left, p 7 (top and bottom right);
Cambridge University Press (from The Decipherment of Linear B,
John Chadwick): p 70;
Eastern Counties Newspapers Ltd: p 14;
French Railways Ltd: p 50;
H J Heinz Company Ltd: p 63 (right);
Philippa Scott: p 72;
Rowntree Mackintosh Ltd: p 122;
Sunday Graphic: p 7;
Syndication International Ltd: p 16, 33.
Grateful thanks also to John Frost, Historical Newspaper Service, for
letting us borrow material for p 6, 7 and 111.

Editors: Beatrice Frei and John West
Layout: Tim Roberts

Kenneth MACKSEY, MC, RTR (ret.) joined the Royal Armoured Corps in 1941 and
continued to serve in the British Army, with tanks and on the Staff, until 1968. He saw
active service in Europe, in India and in the Far East and in this period also
developed as a military writer. When he left the Army he became Deputy Editor of
Purnell's *History of the Second World War* and then of their *History of the First World
War*. So far he has published twenty-one books, the most recent being his biography of
General Guderian. The latest title for Guinness is their *History of Air Warfare, The
Guinness Guide to Feminine Achievements* (in joint authorship with his wife Joan) and
The Guinness Book of 1952 which is the successful predecessor of this title.

Published in Great Britain by
Guinness Superlatives Limited, 2 Cecil Court
London Road, Enfield, Middlesex

ISBN 0 900424 41 9

Guinness is a registered trade mark of
Arthur Guinness Son & Co Ltd

Set in 10 pt. Times and
printed and bound in Great Britain by
Redwood Burn Limited, Trowbridge & Esher

CONTENTS

How leading Cartoonists saw some of the major events of the year

Labour party conference at Margate (News Chronicle, *28 September*) *followed by . . .*

Malenkov succeeded Stalin as premier of the Soviet Union (Daily Express)

. . . The Conservative Party Conference (News Chronicle, *8 October*)

. . . And the United Nations will not waver in their defence of North Korea against the unprovoked aggression of the south (Daily Express)

Any Old Bones? (Daily Mail)

"Suppose the Stewards will take a dim view of any other jockey caught trying to-morrow, eh, Guv?"
(Evening News)

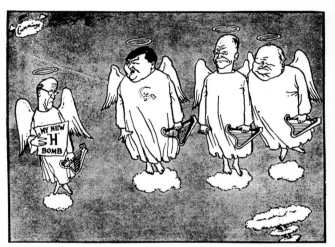

There I told you to stop fiddling with that bomb, comrade professor (Daily Express)

On Coronation day, for the first time in British TV history, more people were watching television than were listening to sound broadcasting (Sunday Graphic)

"Now YOU take the ashes, old boy!"
(Evening Standard)

INTRODUCTION

Whereas 1951 and 1952 had been years of anxiety – unalleviated by, it seemed, any real prospect of improvement in the immediate future – 1953 suddenly and unexpectedly blossomed forth as a year of burgeoning prosperity.

Greater economic stability resulted in a fall in the rate of inflation and in the number of unemployed – a cheerful turn of events highlighted by the colourful pageantry which characterised the Coronation of Queen Elizabeth II.

A further opportunity for patriotic rejoicing was afforded by the happily concomitant triumph of the conquest of Mount Everest.

Sporting events brought many long-awaited successes: In May Stanley Matthews finally took home an FA Cup winner's medal; in June Gordon Richards won the Derby at his 28th attempt, to be followed in August by England's victory in the Ashes for the first time since 1934.

A mood of euphoria descended upon the country, obscuring less agreeable events such as those in British Guiana, Kenya, Trieste and, not least, in Siberia, where the USSR detonated its first hydrogen bomb.

Although some commentators pointed to the need for the nation to seize fresh opportunities and warned that idleness would lead the way to future decline, the population at large preferred to live in the present – content in the knowledge that the war in Korea was over and that food rationing was at last coming to an end.

In 1953 Britain still held a prominent position in world affairs and could boast of strong armed forces, the leadership of a still great Commonwealth and the reputation of being a leading industrial power.

The nature and extent of the changes which would be brought about by the future course of world events, and the drastic effect which these would have on the nation's prestige, were matters which were overlooked in the mood of optimism which prevailed in the country 25 years ago.

SECTION 1

THE HEADLINES

If the valedictory message of 1952 in Britain and in many other nations, too, had been one of hope in the future, linked to the phasing out of the policy of Austerity and financial stringency, the call for 1953, in the eyes of many people besides those of the British Commonwealth, was of a desire to raise standards.

The Presidents change

The eyes of the world were focused on the USA at the beginning of the year, as the transfer of power from **President Harry S Truman** to **Dwight D Eisenhower** entered its

Dwight D Eisenhower is sworn in as President of the USA by Chief Justice Frederick Vinson: Front row left: *former President Harry S Truman and,* right: *Vice President Richard M Nixon*

final stages, culminating in the inauguration on 20 January of the first Republican President in 20 years. For the last time President Truman presented, on 8 January, his budget with its forecast of revenue up to $68 700 million (with no decreases in taxation) against estimated expenditure of $78 600 million; and on the 14th and 15th he gave Congress optimistic reports for the future, foretelling economic prosperity and peace – atomic peace that is – in a world brought closer to a sense of tranquillity by an easing in Soviet Russia's policies. Scarcely could he have guessed that the one event which would cause just such a relaxation was but seven weeks thence. Yet already **Josef Stalin** had intimated that he would be ready to meet the new President, and **Winston Churchill**, Britain's Prime Minister, had travelled to the USA for a 'purely social call' on Eisenhower on 5 January which took the form of prolonged talks lasting until the 7th.

There were no surprises in Eisenhower's inaugural address. Foreign policy was to be along the lines of his predecessors: firm in determination to resist aggression, but linked to an electoral promise that the war in Korea would be brought to an end, and that the Seventh Fleet would no longer be used to defend **Chiang Kai Shek**'s Nationalist China stronghold on Formosa against the mainland Communist Chinese State under **Mao Tse Tung.** On the 27th his Secretary of State, **John Foster Dulles,** filled in the gaps by pointing out that the USA rejected preventive wars but would introduce schemes to encourage the 800 million people under Communist domination to strive for freedom. At the same time he warned of the dangers of Communist infiltration of the Middle East with its vital stocks of oil.

The principal shocks related to Eisenhower's assumption of power were of a more local nature. When it was demanded of **Charles Wilson,** the Secretary of Defence designate, that he sell his large holding of General Motors stock, he objected because he would sustain a substantial loss. In an unguarded moment, he made the celebrated remark, 'What is good for the country is good for General Motors, and vice versa', to which **Adlai Stevenson,** who had been defeated for President, piquantly said, that he did not believe 'General Welfare had become a subsidiary of General Motors'. Wilson sold, however, and got the job. Observing them all was the demagogic personality of Senator **Joseph McCarthy** whose anti-anti-American activities persisted at full power to the extent that he took a hand in attempting to block the appointment by Dulles of **Charles Bohlen** as Ambassador to Russia on the grounds that Bohlen's qualifications were inadequate. Though McCarthy still wielded much influence, he was increasingly the subject of attacks upon himself by others. Eisenhower and Dulles were able to defeat him on the Bohlen issue and he was harmed when, without informing the President and State Secretary, he persuaded certain Greek shipowners to desist from trading with Communist China. On this occasion it was Dulles who came to his rescue, on the grounds that the Senator from Wisconsin had acted '. . . in the national interest', but repugnance at bullying methods was mounting to a climax.

Nevertheless, it would not pass notice that, by the end of the year, in so far as Eisenhower's internal policies were concerned, little or no progress had been made. Already it was becoming plain that a great President had

been succeeded by one of mediocre calibre, one who had ridden to power chiefly on the bandwaggon of the glamorous popularity that his wartime achievements and sympathetic personality had generated.

Cold Wars and Colonial Confrontations

French soldiers on the defensive in Indo-China

Apart from **the Korean War,** there were hot spots of the cold war to be found throughout the Far East (notably in **Malaya** and **Indo-China**), in **Kenya** and in some of the Arab states, particularly in **Egypt** and **Jordan.** With the exception of French Indo-China, British troops were involved and in all the affected areas, again with the exception of Indo-China, the security forces were winning. For, whereas the dissidents in Indo-China could be supplied and reinforced from an adjoining friendly state, China, those in the British territories were cut off from the outside world. They could only live off the countryside by coercion of populaces which were not necessarily supporters of their cause.

In **Indo-China** the Communist **Vietminh** was on the offensive, launching an invasion of Laos in April which the French countered with a parachute landing in the Plain of Jars and at Luang-Prabang. Diplomatic activity was intense as the French endeavoured to lead the independent states into a unified commitment against Communism. But the Vietnamese were intransigent and the **King of Cambodia, Norodom Sihanouk,** evasive until he was granted the independence terms upon which he insisted. On 20 November, at the culmination of a year's unremitting but inconclusive political manoeuvre and battle, the French **General Henri Navarre** committed 15 000 troops, mostly parachutists and Foreign Légionnaires, to the occupation of the village of **Dien-Bien-Phu.** Supplied by air in this fortified zone, it was hoped to disrupt the Vietminh land supply lines and perhaps bring them to a decisive battle. The challenge was gratefully accepted by **General V O Nguyen Giap** who sent four divisions to attack the French forces. Confidently his political chief, **Ho-Chi-Minh,** had announced, 'We are for peace, but peace is impossible without victory.' In response **Richard Nixon,** the American Vice-President, when on a visit in October to Indo-China said, 'there must be no peace negotiations leading to slavery'. But the battle was rising to its height and things did not look too well for the French.

That October in Malaya, however, the British **General Sir Gerald Templer** was able to report a sharp decline in Communist terrorist activity and rising confidence in the country where his efforts, as High Commissioner, to gain the support of the indigenous Malayan, Chinese and Indian people were making headway. Systematic denial of food supplies to the terrorists and a series of minor successes in combat, some by SAS parties parachuted into the jungle, had put the security forces on top. It was claimed that, since the Emergency began in June 1948, 9003 Communist Party members had been accounted for, of whom half were killed, whereas losses to the security forces had been light.

A similar pattern was to be discerned in **Kenya** where the depredations of the **Mau Mau** terrorists of the Kikuyu tribe were being contained. **Jomo Kenyatta,** the Kikuyu leader, who had been put on trial in 1952, was sentenced to seven years hard labour in April, a month after his successor, **F Odede,** had been arrested, and only a few weeks before their Kenya African Union party was suppressed. In the meantime the British Government initiated local elections by secret ballot which were intended to lead the way to a future democracy as part of a reconstituted national Government. As for the terrorists, their activities declined as more British troops arrived, under the command of **Sir George Erskine,** and they were driven into the forests of the Aberdare Range where they were denied food and ruthlessly hunted.

British SAS troops rope down into the Malayan jungle

Kikuyu tribeswomen being dispersed by the police after marching on a police station in Kenya

In **Egypt** the tensions of 1952 with Britain were somewhat relaxed in 1953 because of the internal difficulties being experienced by the government of General **Mohammed Neguib,** and also because genuine negotiations were in progress to reduce or remove the presence of British troops while arranging for the maintenance of the great Base which had been constructed, for the most part, during the war. Subversion by opposition parties prompted Neguib on 10 February to assume supreme powers, but the trial of cases of corruption were only a sop to deflect public attention from the shaky economy.

Another cause of tension in the Middle East was, of course, the continuing state of hostilities between **Israel** and her Arab neighbours. A formal peace had yet to be concluded and there were frequent frontier skirmishes. The use of German credits gave extensive economic support to Israel but Soviet Russia remained hostile. Skirmishing came to a climax on 14 October, when the Israelis launched a surprise punitive raid on the Jordanian villages of Qibya, Budrus and Shuqba. Guerilla bands drawn from settlers whose lives had been imperilled over the months, struck by night, killing 53 Arabs and blowing up 40 houses. The matter was taken to the Security Council of the UN which censured Israel and instructed the Truce Organisation to find ways of strengthening security along the frontier.

Catastrophic flooding by the North Sea

The sea sweeps through homes at Sea Palling, Norfolk, after the catastrophic floods

A malignant combination of three factors conspired, on 31 January, to bring about **the worst disaster of the year.** Northerly winds of over 100 mph (160 km/h) (at 113 mph among the highest ever recorded until then in Britain), a spring tide and an unpredictable tidal surge of 7 feet (2 m) (resulting from barometric pressure), caused great waves to roll down upon the coasts of Holland, Belgium and Britain breaching the sea defences and sweeping inland. By far the worst effects were felt in **Holland** where 145 000 hectares (358 295 acres) were flooded, 1794 people drowned, nearly 100 000 made in need of evacuation, about 50 000 houses destroyed or

A woman of Sutton in Lincolnshire surveys the sand piled up against her front door after the floods had receded

Dutch troops with a DUKW evacuate the people of Raamsdonkveer

damaged, at a total cost estimated at Fl 1000 million. Enormous holes were torn in the dykes, in particular those of the islands of Schouwen, Overflakee, Walcheren, Tholen and the Bevelands. The long Moerdijk bridge was damaged, Rotterdam and Dordrecht flooded: it would be the autumn before all the major damage to the sea defences would be repaired and many years before the full after effects to the land were overcome. In **Belgium,** where only 27 people died, most of the coastal regions were damaged or flooded, as were parts of Antwerp.

In **Britain** where the weather forecast gave little hint of what was impending, it was the coast line from the Humber to the Thames estuary that was hardest hit, although the gales did widespread damage elsewhere. In East Anglia rivers burst their banks, the sea defences at Hunstanton, Heacham and Snettisham broken, and King's Lynn inundated by the tidal surge, just to mention some of the more terrible events on a night in which Canvey Island was flooded and Margate harbour lighthouse destroyed. The toll in lives was put at 307 with 400 houses damaged beyond repair, out of 25 000 affected. A bill of about £50 million was estimated when the initial damages had been assessed. A further disaster that night was the sinking in the Irish Sea of the M V *Princess Vic-*

toria, carrying cars as well as passengers *en route* from Stranraer to Larne. Caught by high (but not abnormal) waves which smashed the stern loading doors (defects in which had been well known for some time), she went down with 133 passengers and crew. Responsibility was placed later on the British Transport Commission and the shipping managers, who were found guilty of poor organisation in maintenance. That same night, too, a trawler was sunk with its crew of 15.

In response to the distress calls from the disaster areas a vast rescue and relief operation went into action. Helicopters from the USA and Switzerland joined with those of the affected countries to lift people from roof tops and land cut off, while every sort of shallow draught boat was pressed into service. To aid the overwhelmed civil authorities, contingents from the armed services from all over Europe were sent to make temporary repairs to repel the next spell of high water. Plans were quickly made to carry out permanent restoration and thus to improve the sea defences so that nothing so drastic could happen again. Claims for financial compensation deluged upon governments and relief funds were opened to help fill the immediate needs of some people who had lost everything they possessed.

The death of Josef Stalin

On 5 March there occurred the most portentous event of the year. The death of **Josef Stalin,** at the age of 73, the Soviet head of state who had been a dominant figure in world as well as national politics for three decades, gave a shock of hope and fear. How many millions of people had died as a result of his policies, what the world's future might have been if he had not been successful in leading Soviet resistance against the Germans during the war, or how much more relaxed the world might have been since 1945, had he not been in power, were questions which crossed the mind that day. Deep in the thoughts of many lay questions concerning the future course of Soviet

policy and the direction the Cold War would now take. The outward calm of the take-over of power by **Georgi Malenkov** gave no hint of the struggle which was instantly triggered within the Kremlin. The unfortunately related death of the President of the Communist Czechoslovakian Republic, **Klement Gottwald,** as the result of pneumonia caught at Stalin's grave side, was but one accidental harbinger of the liquidations to come.

Almost immediately, however, and despite the unexplained shooting down of a RAF Lincoln bomber over Germany on 17 March, there were signs of a relaxation by the Soviets in both external and internal affairs. The

Daily Mirror

FRI MAR. 6 1953

1½d

No. 15,337

Registered at G.P.O. as a Newspaper.

FORWARD WITH THE PEOPLE

CROCODILE TEARS

Stalin dead —OFFICIAL

HOW MOSCOW ANNOUNCED THE END. SEE BACK PAGE

MR. CHURCHILL, the Prime Minister, sends his "regret and sympathy."

Mr. Attlee, the Leader of the Opposition, sends his "sympathy and anxiety."

Mr. R. A. Butler, the Chancellor of the Exchequer, says he is "sorry to hear the news."

Alone among these cautious condolences, President Eisenhower extends "the thoughts of America to all the peoples of the Soviet Union, the men and women, boys and girls, in the villages, cities, farms and factories of their homeland" and expresses his wish for peace to "Russia's millions sharing our longing for a friendly world."

by Cassandra

The President does not praise Marshal Stalin.

Nor does he join the formal diplomatic sorrow. But the glycerine tears go on and the cardboard mourning and the sawdust grief is pumped out non-stop.

I am made of much more callous stuff. I have no regret for Mr. S. I have no sympathy for Mr. S.

And I am not in the slightest bit sorry to hear the latest news about Mr. S.

So granite-hearted am I about J. V. Stalin that I feel not the faintest twinge of grief over the Secretary of the Central Committee of the Communist Party of the Soviet Union.

'Downright Pleased'

There's uncouth indifference for you! But I'll tell you a funny thing. I met another man who's just as bad.

Not only did he not feel regret, sympathy and anxiety, but he was downright pleased.

He said that the news had made the day for him and that he proposed to have a drink on it. I was just pondering on man's inhumanity to man when I met someone else with a tremendous grin lighting up his face until it glowed with sheer warm pleasure.

He was positively gloating over the symptoms. This character was actually rejoicing over the desperate nature of Stalin's illness.

I Found No Grief

He was joined by another chap who remarked brutally that it was the best news he had had since petrol rationing ceased.

I must move in singularly hardened circles. Out of at least a hundred people who have mentioned the matter, not a single one expressed grief.

They weren't grateful to the great Russian for his immense kindnesses in Eastern Europe which are now sending refugees swooning with pure joy into Western Berlin at the rate of nearly 3,000 a day.

They weren't delighted with his wise and kindly role in Malaya and Korea and Indo-China. And

Continued on Back Page

NO HINT OF A SUCCESSOR

IN the long bulletin announcing the death of Stalin no suggestion was made of a successor.

The death announcement was not signed personally by any of the Russian leaders, but jointly by the Central Committee of the Communist Party, the Council of Ministers, and the Praesidium of the Supreme Council.

Young Mr. Wilding faces a camera

EIGHT weeks old and already making a public appearance—that's Michael, son of screen stars Elizabeth Taylor and Michael Wilding. The baby, born in California, U.S., is seen above with his twenty-one-year-old mother in the first picture of them together.

A page of contrasts from the Daily Mirror

Stalin is borne to his granite tomb in Red Square, Moscow, by (left to right in view) *N Shvernik, L Kagonovitch, N Bulganin, V Molotov, V Stalin (son), G Malenkov and L Beria*

fact was that the resolution of a power struggle among the ruling hierarchy of Malenkov, **Lavrenti Beria** of the State Police and **Nikita Khrushchev** (to name the principal contenders only) took priority over all else. Towards the end of March a shift in policy was exposed by the denouncement of **'the cult of individuality'** which had dominated the Stalin regime. Then in April there was a sensational exposure of a plot by doctors who were said to have murdered two minor politicians. This, as it turned out, was merely a trumped-up charge aimed at undermin-

ing Beria whose Security Department was later accused of an error in this matter. Be that as it may, collective leadership is usually ephemeral in Soviet politics; Malenkov gave way in March to Khrushchev as head of the Communist Party while Beria was arrested in July, and later tried and executed on 23 December for 'criminal anti-party and anti-state' activities. To the world at large these events were concealed, and only gradually did the story emerge. Of prime importance to thousands of Soviet political prisoners was the announcement of an amnesty in March – an event whose slow actuation has been subsequently and powerfully described in *One Day in the life of Ivan Denisovich* by **Alexander Solzhenitsyn,** who was among them. For the mass of the Soviet people there was an intensive propaganda campaign designed to allay fears of 'disorder and panic' (of which there were none) and the relaxation of a few minor laws along with some economic concessions. To the rest of the world things looked remarkably normal. The Cold War, apart from an ending of the Korean confrontation (see page 25), went on much as before. The stream of propaganda emanating from both sides of the Iron and Bamboo Curtains poured out unabated and the many immigrants went on crossing from the Eastern to the Western side in Germany, for example, where 9 million had arrived since 1945. In China, the Communists were industriously eliminating Western influence as fast as possible by forcing the closure of consulates and arresting some of the few remaining Catholic priests, among others, on charges of espionage; the British were negotiating £15 million worth of trade in June and found themselves embroiled on 9 September when a Chinese warship fired on a naval launch near Hong Kong, killing seven men and wounding five.

Marshal Tito and the Trieste Solution

This disputed territory had been maintained by US and British troops on behalf of the UN as an international demilitarised zone since 1945. At the centre of the debate, on whether it should be returned to Italy or given to Yugoslavia, stood the heroic figure of **Marshal Tito,** himself a symbol of the Cold War. Tito, who had won admiration for his leadership of Yugoslav partisans in the war and had, since then as Head of State, made his dramatic break from Soviet and, above all, Stalinist domination, came to London on a State visit eleven days after Stalin died. He was negotiating for overseas economic aid while engaged at home in a progressive reorganisation of government, with concessions to the peasants. The International Bank would later inject $30 million and the USA a further $46 million into the Yugoslav economy. Although a Russian ambassador was allowed to return to Belgrade in June, Tito made it clear that his country would not rejoin the Soviet bloc. Pro-Western sentiments were sharply set back in October, however, when a surprise joint US–British announcement rejected Tito's proposals that Trieste should become a free port. They

Winston Churchill and Marshal Tito at No. 10 Downing Street

opted, instead, for returning one of its two zones to **Italy** and leaving the other with **Yugoslavia.** Tempers were aroused and demonstrations and riots took place as the two nations made threatening gestures throughout October and November. It was Tito who defused the situation on 29 November by suggesting that troops should be withdrawn from the frontier so that negotiations in a five-power conference could begin in an atmosphere of calm. The Italians concurred.

A facet in the Cod War: the attempt to prevent the sale of fish brought into the country by Mr George Dawson, using untraditional means

Iceland seeks to extend its fishing limits to four miles

This Icelandic proposal, modest by the standards of subsequent years, was made in May and had as its background a clash of party political rivalries allied to internal economic demand and the external diplomatic pressures that were brought to bear on Iceland by the USA and USSR in consequence of her membership of NATO. The British response to any limitation of fishing came, ostensibly, from the ports of Hull and Grimsby which refused to allow Icelandic boats to land their catches there – and Iceland depended on fish for 95% of her exports. When the British Government suggested that the dispute should go to the International Court of Justice, the Icelanders demanded that the ban should first be lifted, but at this the British Foreign Office demurred on the grounds that the ports were a private enterprise, outside its control.

At the Icelandic election in June the Conservatives retained control with an increased majority over the Labour party which had attempted to have the NATO treaty revised to limit the presence of US troops in this vital mid-Atlantic base and to insist that Icelanders be exclusively employed. These disputes now entered the realms of Cold War with the USSR concluding a fish barter agreement worth $12 million in exchange for fuel oil on the understanding that no oil from other sources was to be imported. Meanwhile, the International Bank for Reconstruction advanced two loans to the value of $1½ million. Realising their key position, the Icelandic political parties embarked on a policy of bargaining in Cold War power currencies that persists to this day.

Everest conquered

From the moment man first set eyes on **Everest,** (29 028 feet (8847 m)) he schemed to reach its peak but always his efforts had been defeated – in the previous year the Swiss had failed by only the narrowest of margins. Though there were some in 1952 who had concluded that the mountain would never be climbed, a British expedition under **John Hunt** was making carefully considered preparations to prove them wrong. Hunt's approach was conditioned by his training in systematic Army General Staff planning procedures on the lines that the mountain could not be rushed. Apart from meticulous preparation much depended upon the use of reliable oxygen breathing apparatus, the full importance of which was then debatable. By 8 March the team of British, New Zealand and Nepalese climbers had gathered at Katmandu backed by some 350 porters whose task it was to carry equipment and stores and establish successive supply dumps on the slopes of the mountain. Throughout April and May the steady logistic build-up and advance progressed with military precision until, on 26 May, the first assault party

was within striking distance of the peak. Next day, however, they were repulsed by bad weather. On the 28th the second attempt was ready with a strong party that included **Edmund Hillary** and Sherpa **Tenzing Norgay** established at a height of 28 215 ft (8599 m) poised for the assault on the summit. On the 29th in bitter cold (−15°F (−26°C)) but in conditions that were otherwise quite good, Hillary and Tenzing, each carrying about 65 lb (29 kg), began the final climb, cutting footholds in the ice as they struggled upwards. At 11.30 am they suddenly, and somewhat unexpectedly, found themselves at the top, where they spent 15 minutes taking photographs. Then began the cautious descent down a path that was already partially obscured, to be met at the lower levels by the support parties prior to beating a retreat to the base camp. Ahead sped the news of their triumph, to reach London by radio on the evening of 1 June just in time for the announcement to precede the great event of the following day. Worthily of the occasion the London *Times* was able to declare 'Seldom since Francis Drake brought the *Golden Hind* to anchor in Plymouth Sound has a British explorer offered to his sovereign such a tribute of glory as Colonel John Hunt and his men were able to lay at the feet of Queen Elizabeth for her Coronation'.

The conquerors of Mount Everest, Edmund Hillary and Sherpa Tenzing Norgay

The Coronation of Queen Elizabeth II

Front row: *Prince Michael of Kent
The Duke of Cornwall (Charles; now Prince of Wales)
Princess Anne (m. Capt. Mark Phillips)
Prince Richard of Gloucester
Prince William of Gloucester (k. 1972)*

Second row: *The Duchess of Beaufort
The Hereditary Grand Duchess of Luxembourg
Princess Marie Louise (d. 1956)
Princess Alice, Countess of Athlone
Princess Alexandra of Kent (m. Angus Ogilvie)
The Duchess of Kent (d. 1968)
The Crown Princess of Norway
The Princess Margaret
The Queen
Queen Elizabeth The Queen Mother
The Princess Royal (d. 1965)
The Duchess of Gloucester
Lady Patricia Ramsay (d. 1974)
Countess Mountbatten (d. 1960)
Earl Mountbatten
Lady Pamela Mountbatten (now Hicks)
Lady Brabourne
Princess George of Greece
Prince George of Greece*

Third row: *The Hereditary Grand Duke of Luxembourg
The Prince of Liege
The Duke of Beaufort
Lt. Col. Sir Henry Abel Smith
The Duke of Kent
Lady May Abel Smith
The Crown Prince of Norway
Princess Astrid of Norway
Princess Dorothea of Hesse
The Duke of Edinburgh
The Marchioness of Cambridge
The Duke of Gloucester (d. 1974)
The Earl of Harewood
The Hon. Gerald Lascelles
The Countess of Harewood (now Mrs Jeremy Thorpe)
Captain the Hon. Alexander Ramsay
Admiral The Hon. Sir Alexander Ramsay (d. 1972)
Mr Peter Whitley
Lord Brabourne*

Fourth row: *The Prince Axel of Denmark
Princess Margaretha of Denmark
Prince Kraft of Hohenlohe-Langenburg
The Princess of Hohenlohe-Langenburg (immediately on the right of The Duke of Edinburgh)
The Prince of the Netherlands (Bernhard)
The Margrave of Baden
The Margravine of Baden
Princess Christina of Hesse
The Earl of Athlone (d. 1957)
Prince Max of Baden
The Prince of Hohenlohe-Langenburg*

Family group in the Throne Room of Buckingham Palace after the Coronation.

Throughout the previous year a rising swell of excitement had surged forward at the prospect of the forthcoming Coronation, heavily stimulated by publicity in the press, on radio and television as the great day approached. The illustrated magazines for women and those of wider appeal, such as *Picture Post* and *Illustrated*, had enjoyed a field day while the shops were crammed with souvenirs and the streets became festooned with flags. In the meantime there was a boom in the sale of television sets to enable millions to watch the parades and the whole ceremony 'live' for the first time. In fact it was the weather which did its best to ruin things: it rained intermittently on the crowd of a million people which gathered along the route of the procession throughout the day. The elements, however, failed to dull the parade's magnificence, a cavalcade that took 45 minutes to pass and included thousands of troops from all over the Commonwealth who provided a richly uniformed backcloth to the central players in their robes, coronets and ermine. Oblivious of the rain, the delighted crowd wondered at the sight of the representatives of 72 states including 12 princes and princesses and ten prime ministers, among a mass of nobility, driving past in horse drawn coaches. The dignified beauty of the Queen at the extraordinarily moving instant of Coronation, and her gaiety as she waved from her coach or from the balcony of Buckingham Palace captivated everyone. By far the next most popular 'star' was the ebullient **Queen Salote of Tonga.** At times she seemed in peril of losing her balance as she excitedly rose to the crowd in her own rain swept open coach.

The Queen, supported by the Bishop of Durham and the Bishop of Bath and Wells, approaches enthronement

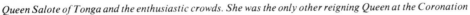

Queen Salote of Tonga and the enthusiastic crowds. She was the only other reigning Queen at the Coronation

Street decorations in the Royal Mile, Edinburgh

A few additional statistics are as follows:
Total crowd in London (estimated) 1 million (including 31 000 children in the stands along the Embankment).

Squadrons of aircraft in fly-past	12
Number of American and Canadian visitors	25–30 000
who were estimated to spend	$17 million
Cost of the event	£2.3 million
Sale of stand tickets	£640 000

Unfortunately, there were 6873 casualties among the crowds, of which 313 necessitated admittance to hospital and several of which proved fatal to people exposed in the streets to the cold and wet weather the night before. Lest it be thought that everything took place in London, it must not be forgotten that every town and village in the land and many throughout the Commonwealth also organised their own functions, such as Street Parties, by way of celebration.

Riots in East Berlin

In sharp contrast to the emotional warmth of the British scene came news of a chill Cold War breeze from **Berlin.** Oppression of the people in the Eastern zone was largely economic but reflected, too, persecution of the Church by the Communist government, heavily influenced by the Soviets. These pressures drove an increasing number of desperate people to cross to the West. On a single day in March no less than 6000 sought asylum in West Berlin (there was no wall in those days) and by May the number that year of those who had found their way from all points to Western Germany, reached 340 000. High taxes, high prices and a dogged insistence by the Communists on high production levels for low pay, induced a spontaneous outburst by the workers who on 16 June went on strike and carried their resistance into the streets of Berlin. Soviet troops and tanks were stoned, the Red Flag flung from the top of the Brandenburger Tor, and fires started by crowds which roamed the streets in a state of outright rebellion. Even members of the people's police – the hated Vopos – joined their ranks and soon there were arms in the rebels' hands. Shooting began while the people of the Western Sector watched and

waited. At midday on the 17th the Soviet military command proclaimed a state of emergency and proceeded by the use of tanks, troops and summary trial and execution to suppress the rioters. By 18 June the crowds had disappeared and it was the Soviets who held the fort with an iron grip which was not to be relaxed until 8 July. In the meantime the death toll, variously put at between 25 and 569, could be matched against a clear indication that outright Communist suppression was not in itself enough to cow a determined people. The East German government was shaken, the Soviets put on their guard and the other satellite nations given a breath of hope – one that was stimulated by the Americans who, in August, began in Berlin to distribute thousands of food parcels to the distressed people of the East who walked across to the Western Sector to collect them. The effect in **Poland,** for example, was good; there **food rationing,** which had been introduced in 1952, had already been cancelled and efforts were made to give the people a better share in wages and food. In the meantime negotiations were in progress to release German prisoners of the Second World War still held by the Soviets. Agreement was reached in August, the first 3500 were set free in October and a further batch on 31 December, bringing the total thus far to 10 369.

In East Berlin Soviet tanks are stoned by rioters

An Armistice in Korea

Signing the Korean Armistice at Panmunjom: left *Lt-Gen William K Harrison of the USA;* right *General Nam Il of North Korea*

At the beginning of the year the armistice negotiations at **Panmunjom** were deadlocked over the single issue of whether or not prisoners of war should be forcibly repatriated or be allowed to make their own choice. For the Communists, with 171 000 of their number in United Nations' hands of which the majority had no wish to return home, a matter of faith and principle was involved. They held but 11 500 non Korean prisoners (though many South Koreans had probably been conscripted into the North Korean Army and had disappeared, and a great many had died) the vast majority of whom wished to be repatriated. The first breakthrough came in February when **General Mark Clark** proposed that sick and wounded prisoners should be exchanged, a suggestion that led to some 6000 Communist and 600 UN soldiers being released in April.

The fighting, in the meantime, went on almost constantly in the air (with nearly 130 000 sorties flown by the UN air forces between 1 January and 31 May) and by fits and starts on the ground whenever the Communists tried to win some sort of prestige success to strengthen their bargaining power at the conference table. There were 22 different attacks in March, a further flurry of activity in May and a large-scale offensive in June which drove South Korean troops back some 2½ miles (4 km) at the very moment when agreement at Panmunjom was close. And on the very eve of an Armistice being signed the Communists launched an intensive artillery attack. The UN forces returned the fire with the result that the casualty toll mounted steeply on both sides. Right until the end, as if to make it clear that they had not given anything away, the Communists kept up the fighting.

Repatriated British prisoners of war from Korea arrive in England

The Communist offensive in June was directly aimed at the South Korean Army because of intransigence on the part of their President, **Syngman Rhee.** At the last moment he had objected to a conclusion to the war on the grounds that Korea was still divided and also to an arrangement that gave the Communists an opportunity to persuade their prisoners to return home. On 18 June, ten days after an agreement on repatriation procedures had been signed, Rhee blandly announced that 25 000 North Korean prisoners had broken out, though later he admitted they had been released on his orders. This delayed

Korea: the dividing line between North and South

negotiations until pressure could be brought to bear on Rhee by Clark to persuade him to agree to the Armistice. At last it was signed on 27 July. On 5 August the exchange of prisoners began and was completed on 6 September, by which time nearly 76 000 Communists had been returned and nearly 13 000 men of the UN. From the UN prisoners came tales of the harsh treatment and indoctrination procedures inflicted on them, particularly on the US troops. As for the Communists, only 3 per cent of those who had refused to return home could be persuaded to change their minds. A war which had cost the UN at least 500 000 dead with over 460 000 missing was over; the armies settled down in the entrenchments of the ceasefire line where they remain 25 years later.

The number of soldiers killed among the principal member states of the UN involved was as follows:

South Korea	415 000
USA	25 604
Turkey	717
Britain	710
Australia	291
Canada	291
France	288

An atomic device is exploded in the Nevada Desert, USA

Russia explodes her H Bomb

The extensive testing of nuclear weapons of various sizes continued throughout the year. On its Nevada ranges, the USA fired **the first atomic shell** from its 280 mm gun to a range of 6¼ miles (10 km) ; at Woomera in Australia the British exploded **their second atomic bomb,** and on 12 August the Russians detonated their **first thermo-nuclear weapon (H Bomb)** a mere nine months after **the first American H device in 1952.** Thus, although the Western Powers retained a substantial lead in the nuclear race with larger and more plentiful weapons and with superior means of delivery, the Eastern bloc was catching up and the days of nuclear parity were in sight. In parallel, the ethical and strategic problems were debated with vigour by the protagonists of pre-emptive war and the disciples of a nuclear deterrent took issue with the growing band of those who demanded nuclear disarmament.

The Crisis in Persia
and the Fall of Dr Mussadiq

In the wake of **Dr Mussadiq**'s triumphs as Persia's Premier over his political opponents at home and over the British in the International Courts on the subject of the Anglo-Iranian Oil Co in 1952, **governmental chaos** and economic collapse threatened the country, most of it stemming from Mussadiq's megalomania and inability to compromise. At odds with the **Shah** over disposal of the

Royal lands – and, indeed, over the Shah's whole position as ruler, he gradually assumed a position in which his main support came from the Communist **Tudeh Party** which based its claim for 'popular' support on the classic posture of promising anything from republicanism to women's emancipation. Ranged against him was a substantial Royalist group, with latent support from liberal, military and landed elements and a vocal opposition in the Majlis (parliament). Obstinately Mussadiq persisted in imposing an inflexible will upon both Shah and Majlis, threatening them respectively with ejection and dissolution. Arbitrarily he dismissed all attempts at reaching an agreement over the oil except on his own terms. Inexorably, shortage of funds drove him, in May, to ask President **Eisenhower** for financial aid, a request which was formally turned down on 9 July. Almost at once his friends in the Majlis began to withdraw support and power began to descend upon the shoulders of General **Zahedi**. On 15 August Zahedi made an abortive attempt to arrest Mussadiq, a failure which prompted the Shah and his queen to flee. Until the 19th Mussadiq, boosted by the Tudeh Party which came out on the streets, held sway, but on the 19th the Army took a hand in whipping up popular support for the Shah, seizing Mussadiq and bringing back the Shah on a wave of hysteria on the 22nd. At once the Americans granted $45 million aid and Zahedi took power with the task of restoring the country's political and economic equilibrium. By the end of the year Mussadiq had been tried for treason and sen-

The Shah of Persia arrives home from his short exile. To his right stands General Zahedi, the new Persian Premier, who made his return possible

tenced to three years in prison, negotiations had begun for the settlement of the oil dispute with a consortium of American, British and Dutch companies, and arrangements were being made to elect a new Majlis early in 1954.

Disturbances
in British Guiana and Morocco

In any survey of 1953 (and almost any other year in the 1950s, for that matter) it has to be appreciated that in almost every country, though more noticeably among the politically backward ones, the road to progress was littered with confrontations, violent and non-violent. Typical examples were provided by **British Guiana** and **Morocco. British Guiana** was well on the way from colonial type rule to a working constitution in 1953 and elections were held in April. Unfortunately for the composure of the British Government and the Western hemisphere powers, the electorate voted 18 seats out of 24 to the People's Progressive Party, led by Dr **Cheddi Jagan,** an East Indian, which had pronounced Communist tendencies. He became *de facto* prime minister and his American born wife, **Janet,** the PPP's secretary, deputy speaker. Following a series of strikes in September the British sent in troops and naval forces in October, denounced Jagan's demands for nationalisation of industry and the abolition of the Governor's reserved powers, and suspended the new constitution – a suspension that was to last until 1957.

In **Morocco** it was the French who were at the centre of a colonial balancing act between their resident nationals and the indigenous population under their progressive **Sultan** whose desire was independence for his country. In August the French deposed Sultan **Mohammed ben Yussef** and replaced him with his uncle, **Mulay Arafa,** saying that it was he who enjoyed popular support – a claim that had little foundation in fact. The proscribed Istiqlal party, from which the deposed Sultan drew his policy, announced that they were at war with the French and on 11 September an attempt was made on the life of Mulay Arafa. To the credit of the new Sultan he, in collaboration with the French, initiated electoral and judical reforms and the dismantling of antique court procedures in order to modernise the sultanate. But as a force to be reckoned with he was a novice by comparison with the man he had helped to depose; and so the seeds of change were sown.

The scene during the assassination attempt on the Sultan of Morocco at Rabat

Above: *RAF Lincoln bombers fly past the Queen at Odiham, Hants. In the biggest fly-past in the history of the Royal Air Force more than 640 planes took part.*

Below: *Queen Elizabeth II reviews her Fleet at Spithead*

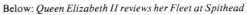

The Royal Reviews and Tours

An extended and almost exhausting round of tours and visits was planned for the Queen and members of the Royal Family in the months following the Coronation. The **Trooping of the Colour** was of importance but, for the grandest scale, the **Naval Review** at Spithead had to be seen on 15 June when the Queen in the Royal Yacht *Surprise* sailed through a fleet of 200 ships that included the last British battleship, HMS *Vanguard*, nine aircraft carriers, ten cruisers and ships from 16 foreign navies including those of the USA, USSR and France. Never again would so large a fleet be assembled in Home Waters as this Spithead assemblage. A month later it was the turn of the **Royal Air Force** at Odiham where 4000 men and 318 aircraft paraded on the ground for their Queen and 641 planes of 30 different types flew past. Watching them, too, was the **Duke of Edinburgh** who had himself qualified as a pilot on 4 May. In the meantime there had been four drives by the Queen through London, an extensive tour of Scotland, a visit to Northern Ireland and to Wales and plans were well advanced for the most ambitious tour of all. Starting on 23 November, this would last for six months and take the Royal Party by land, air and sea to many parts of the Commonwealth.

The route lay through the Panama Canal in the liner *Gothic* to the West Indies and then across the Pacific Ocean to **Fiji.**

Then on to New Zealand where the Queen spent Christmas (and gave her annual radio broadcast) and New Year's Day. Vast crowds, that included thousands of children in addition to the ebullient **Queen Salote of Tonga** and great statesmen, came out to give a great and tumultuous welcome. These were the days before such tours had become routine and had lost their mystery and splendour.

The Great Treaties
and Mr Dulles's 'Agonising reappraisal'

Behind each of the major pacts and alliances governing anti-communist defence lay the material and economic support of the USA. The **North Atlantic Treaty Organisation** (NATO) which had been in being since 1948, the **Anzus pact** which had been signed in 1952 and that for the **European Defence Community** (EDC) which had been signed in 1952 but had yet to be ratified by all the signatories in 1953, placed an annual expenditure of $78 billion on that nation, of which the following items had a bearing on defence or the aid to her associated nations:

	$
Atomic Energy Commission	1 802 411 828
Defence Production expansion	87 119 559
Mutual Security Programme	5 551 237 228
Defence Department	44 352 427 640
Strategic and Critical Material	912 086 377

By way of comparison, Britain's defence expenditure was £1636 million (about $4580 million) and NATO's defence expenditure some $63 500 million to which the USA made by far the largest contribution.

It was with these figures in mind, balanced against the need to out-face the Communist bloc, that **John Foster Dulles** entered office as US State Secretary with the intention of containing his country's commitment, getting value for its money and making effective existing and future treaties. By the end of the year he had travelled throughout Europe, Turkey, the Middle East, Pakistan, India and the Far East, including Korea. On the one hand he was endeavouring to bring about a Summit Conference of the so-called **'Big-Four'** – the USA, Britain, USSR and France – with China excluded. On the other Foster Dulles was trying to make the EDC and its associated European Army, which included a German contingent, a reality. Frequently he was in the headlines, just as a later Secretary, Dr Kissinger, so often would be, and like Kissinger he was not always able to obtain the results he desired. He managed to persuade the British to cease trading in strategic goods with China and he signed a mutual defence pact with the South Koreans, but in December he could see that EDC was in danger of rejection, largely as the result of reticence on the part of the Italians and, above all, the French who did not wish to be deprived of their armed forces for use in their overseas territories. Each nation managed to introduce some nationalistic stipulation as a condition of ratification until, on 14 December, Dulles lost patience and said, in a celebrated remark, that unless ratification of EDC was soon forthcoming his Government would be forced to make 'an agonising reappraisal' of its policies. At the end of the year, however, EDC was no closer to realisation.

John Foster Dulles, waving to a group of Londoners upon his arrival at the Foreign Office

Above: *Meeting in New Delhi of the Pakistani and Indian leaders:* left to right, *HE Sir Mohd. Zafrullah Khan, Shrimati Vijayalakshmi Pandit, Begum Mohammed Ali, Dr Rajendra Prasad, HE Mr Mohammed Ali, Prime Minister of Pakistan, and the Indian Prime Minister Jawaharlal Nehru*

Pakistan to become a Republic

Under the severe economic pressure arising out of the fall in commodity prices in 1952, a programme of constitutional reform was carried out in Pakistan. **Mohammed Ali** became Prime Minister in April, his first task being to widen the scope of the electoral system to give overall representation to both West and East (now Bangladesh) Pakistan. These proposals when presented on 2 November, foreshadowed the conversion of the country to a republic. Simultaneously strenuous efforts were made to settle the quarrels with **India** over trade arrangements and, of course, the matter of **Kashmir.** Visits by Mohammed Ali to India and by the Indian Prime Minister, **Jawaharlal Nehru,** to Pakistan were resounding successes, coming as they did in the aftermath of a June meeting of Commonwealth Prime Ministers in London at which Nehru had played a prominent part. However, at the end of December the two sides were still deadlocked in the attempt to arrange a plebiscite over Kashmir.

Below: Dr Jonas Salk, discoverer of a polio vaccine

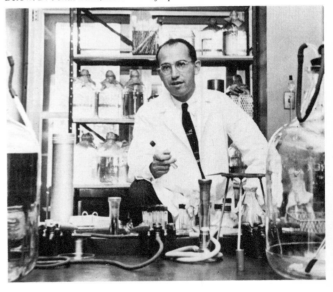

A vaccine against polio

Although the prevalence of **poliomyelitis** (infantile paralysis) was much lower in most parts of the world than it had been in 1952, interest in its isolation and control was substantial. At the University of California **Dr Wendell Stanley** announced that the virus had been identified. Meanwhile two kinds of vaccine were under test; the gamma globulin developed by **Dr William Hammon** and his team at the University of Pittsburgh, which had been under test in 1952 and which seemed to give a partial protection (though the World Health Organisation denied it), and that of **Dr Jonas Salk** and his team, of the same university, which consisted of a combination of three types of poliovirus strains inactivated by treatment with formalin. Both were due for intensive investigation the following year and it would be Salk's vaccine which, in 1955, would bring the most impressive reduction in a disease which was so frequently headline news because of its damaging effects on people, the young in particular.

At the end of the year

There was, as usual, a note of hope on the front pages. For the world in general a slight easing of tensions and an improvement in the economic situation gave reason for optimism. There was, perhaps, a deeper significance than usual in the fact that two Nobel Peace Prizes were awarded this year, one retrospectively to **Dr Albert Schweitzer** (German), to compensate for the decision to omit this award in 1952, and the other, for 1953, to **George Marshall** (USA). Both were legendary figures. Schweitzer was renowned for his prowess as a philospher, theologian, musician and physician and as founder of the famous leprosy mission station at Lambaréné in French Equatorial Africa. Marshall was the most revered of American Chiefs of Staff, the man who had prepared the US Army for war and guided its strategy under Franklin Roosevelt throughout the Second World War and who had been US Ambassador to China before his appointment as Secretary of State by Harry Truman in 1947. It was in this latter capacity that Marshall had headed the vast scheme which had made possible the quicker recovery of Europe in the aftermath of war and which was known as the Marshall Plan.

In the USA there was real prosperity with reduced controls, and in Britain the end of food rationing was at last in sight with the announcement that a new ration book was not to be printed for the next rationing year beginning in May 1954. Moreover, 11 000 tons of canned corned beef were released off ration in June, meat was derationed in August, and the bakers were allowed to make white bread again. But for the British, in a year of

Dr Albert Schweitzer at the age of 78

pageantry and splendour, the warning given by *The Times* in its leader on the day after the Coronation went largely unheeded: they had enjoyed, it said, '. . . a holiday from reality long enough . . .' and 'A country made great by resourcefulness and energy is slowly strangling itself with restrictive practices . . . and by a plain disinclination for hard work'.

Christmas morning at Government House, New Zealand

SECTION 2
THE EVERYDAY SCENE

The Weather

Unlike the preceding year, 1953's weather was moderate in Europe (apart from the end of January (see page 14) though, as usual, it was prone to violent caprices in the USA, where, for example, the occasional tornado struck the central region in May and the drought (June was the driest since 1871) ruined the crops of the south-west later in the year. Too much of the suffocatingly dangerous **'smog'** which the British had suffered, with fatal consequences for many, late in 1952, or too little rain were subjects that made headline news and therefore promoted discussions about remedies.

In Britain a Committee of Air Pollution was set up to study the causes of 'smog' – which had also affected New York for an eight-day spell in November; in due course its findings brought about measures to control the use of smoky fuels, a task as yet incomplete 25 years later, but which was then launched as a project to try out **'smokeless zones'** in London. As for rainmaking, nobody in authority was prepared to rate it feasible, pointing out that, although for years there had been talk of 'seeding' clouds with dry ice, there was always the necessity of having clouds to seed. Nevertheless, President Eisenhower set up a Federal Weather Control Commission in August and its deliberations went on to a background of gossip that every abnormality was caused by atomic explosions.

The dissemination of news

Though television as an industry was very much on the increase (see page 59) it was still less important in spreading news, comment, and advertising than the traditional newspapers, periodicals and radio.

In Britain newspapers cost about 1½d (1p) and were being allowed to increase in size as controls gradually were lifted from the supply of newsprint. Among 164 dailies the *Daily Mirror*, with an average daily circulation

A smog mask on sale in Boots

The record breaking Coronation Day issue of the Daily Mirror

during the year of 4½ million, **set up a world record by sel-ling** 7 million copies on Coronation Day, and the *Daily Graphic,* which changed its name to *Daily Sketch,* also raised its sales. Meanwhile a Canadian, **Roy Thomson,** bought Scotsman Publications Ltd. Of the weekly pictorials, *Picture Post* and *Illustrated* were dominant in an industry which produced 1369 weekly newspapers and 3844 periodicals. The formation of an advisory **Press Council** was a major attempt at raising standards. As for the radio broadcasting of news, people continued to listen faithfully to the well-established six and nine o'clock BBC summaries, the style and integrity of which had changed but little since the war, while overseas broadcasting, though curtailed, was still prolific.

France lost a few newspapers of Communist inclination through lack of support, and there were several mergers to compete with rising costs and declining circulations, a pattern that was to be discerned in **Italy** and elsewhere. In **Western Germany,** however, **Axel Springer,** who owned 10 per cent of the country's newspapers and periodicals, bought *Die Welt* from the British High Commissioner's department.

In **the USA** a complete overhaul of the Government radio information service, **Voice of America,** led to an extensive cut back in funds and a halt on expansion. In August it came under State Department control. Meanwhile the newspaper industry, which printed the traditionally jumbo-sized editions, was running into serious competition from television and its profits were lower than at any time since 1946. Circulation of English language daily editions remained steady at about 54½ million with weekly periodicals rising to 17½ million, of which *Life*, at 5 311 747, topped the bill. But the weekly magazine with the **largest world circulation** was *Readers Digest* at a little over 17 million.

Employment

The number of people engaged in different kinds of employment varied substantially between nations. Statistics for Britain and the USA with their mixed economies were as follows at mid-year:

	Britain (000)	USA (000)
Agriculture and Fishing	1107	10 000
Civil Government Service	1318	6638
Mining and Quarrying	869	837
Public Utilities	374	
Transport and Communications	1723	4312
Manufacturing	8852	17 155
Building etc	1452	2584
Distributive Trades	2660	10 401
Professional and Financial Services	3970	7445
Military Service	864	3304
Unemployed	299	1562

The figures represented a marked improvement over those of 1952 in that far fewer people were unemployed, a state of affairs that was dramatically noticeable in Western Germany where, despite the influx of refugees from the eastern sector, the number of unemployed had dropped from 1 432 000 in 1951 to the million mark. At the same time a people who were becoming obsessed by what was to become known as the 'work-storm', were rapidly increasing production while holding down the cost of living. It was about the same in the USA where the cost of living rose by 1 per cent and wages by 7.4 per cent and in Britain where the cost of living rose by about 4 per cent with wages up 5 per cent.

Krupp's training scheme for youngsters: German youths wearing typical German Army hats undergoing training

A reduction in the size of wage demands not unnaturally had a tranquillising effect upon labour relations and so the number of strikes, though quite frequent in the USA, lost far fewer working days than in the previous year. Likewise in Britain, where two strikes only were of serious impact, there was a sense of peace. That by the **Electrical Trades Union** for a 3d (1.25p) per hour wage increase (which the employers refused) was interesting because its Communist dominated executive chose to use the union's new constitution to call out selected members without resort to balloting, as hitherto. Beginning on 24 August men were called out at those places where most harm could result, including atomic plants; but on 17 September the union acceded to a request to start work prior to attending a court of inquiry which, in October, managed to make both sides use the recognised negotiating procedures. On 20 October 2500 **oil company drivers** stopped work in support of a wage claim. Within three days there was serious shortage of fuel at garages. The Minister of Labour, **Sir Walter Monkton,** called out troops who quickly restored adequate supplies. Other unions were unsympathetic and the strike collapsed on the 26th. In France strikes by miners, municipal and transport workers were aimed at the Government's attempt to reform the terms of employment with the result that a weak Government backed down (see page 45).

Troops being employed to break the unofficial strike of London petrol tanker drivers. Over 2700 troops began to take a fleet of 700 tankers to 50 petrol depots in the London area

Wage rates and prices

Though the rate of increase in wages and prices was lower than in 1952, there was still a rise throughout the world which was reflected in Britain and the USA. In France, however, the rise was steeper than average, but the cost of living index in Germany actually fell. (See below).

In Britain the **weekly expenditure on food** by a family of four (still somewhat restricted by rationing) was about £4 5s (£4.25), slightly up on 1952, while in the USA it remained at about $20 though with more to spend it on. **Beer** in Britain cost about 1s 2d (6p) a pint, and **rents** curbed by the Rent Restrictions Act of 1939, remained steady, 12s 6d (62½p) being the typical weekly rent for a council house. Private rents, however, were due for revision by a Conservative Government which was anxious about the deterioration of property due to too low a rent being permitted. **Income Tax** in Britain was reduced from 9s 6d (47½p) to 9s (45p) in the £1; a married couple with one child and an annual income of £1000 might pay £139. In **West Germany,** however, where a General Election was impending, a reduction of 15 per cent was made in Income Tax.

Compulsory Military Service remained, of course, the rule rather than the exception for most nations, with hardly a family that did not have some member or other in uniform and some which had even suffered the loss of a son. In the USA selective military service (**The Draft**) still operated, with about half a million draftees a year putting

Jack Jones of the Transport Workers Union, outside the Labour Exchange in Coventry on a Friday afternoon

on uniform. In Britain most able-bodied men were called up for two years. In USSR and China service in the armed forces was virtually universal with millions under some form of training well into middle age.

Weekly Wages	Agricultural Worker	Coal Miner	Manufacturing Worker	Average Wage
Britain	£6	£13	£9 6s (£9.30)	£7 11s (£7.55)
USA	$50	$90	$72	$70

Populations and migration

According to the latest census figures, **the estimated world's population** stood at 2 438 369 000. By continents, this was as below:

Africa	190 820 000
Antarctica	Zero
Asia	1 296 881 000
Australasia and Oceania	13 349 000
Europe	403 831 000
North America	225 437 000
South America	113 051 000
USSR	201 300 000

(not included in Asia and Europe above)

Apart from the movement of large numbers from **East into West Germany** (see page 34 above), this was a year of reduced migration with those nations, such as **Australia,** which had been previously encouraging it, lowering their quotas owing to lack of facilities for immigrants.

The German Red Cross distributes food to refugees in Berlin

Holidays

Within each country the traditional ways of holiday making persisted, virtually unchanged by the increasing ease of transport and a gradual loosening of frontier restrictions. The existence of the Iron Curtain, of course, made travel to Communist countries extremely difficult, but in Europe passports were no longer necessary between **France** and the **Benelux** countries, for example, while **currency allowances** were raised in the case of the British to £50 per adult in November. Peak periods remained substantially the same, too, conditioned by weather and school holidays with, in Britain, a preference for the static seaside stay in boarding houses or holiday camps. Efforts to change people's habits were a failure. Nevertheless, the greater number of motor cars and motor cycles available were taking people farther afield and more were persuaded to go camping or caravaning as part of a mobile holiday. As a result the hoteliers were noticing the difference. While a 13-day holiday in Scotland was advertised at £37 17s (£37.85), a 17-day Grand Tour of Yugoslavia cost only £51 9s (£51.45). The

Holiday time in Mablethorpe, Lincs, six months after the flood

package tour was getting under way though as yet the mode of travel was more often on the surface than in the air. Tourists poured into Europe from North America – some 400 000 Americans alone – and Britain took in the then record of 810 000 from all nations who spent £125 million, of which £47 million was in dollars. The widespread introduction of tourist air flights, which had started in 1952, now began to open up the possibilities of holidays in distant parts as never before.

The launching by the American Hotel Credit Corporation of **hotel credit cards** was a scheme that achieved only partial success in helping travellers to pay more easily, but was just one aspect of the travel industry of the USA which made very determined efforts to encourage holiday makers as well as business men. In Europe, the 'motel' (already well established in the USA) was beginning to appear. **The Royal Oak** at Hythe in Kent, was the first to open in Britain.

Above: *Juno, June, Jean and Janet, the first lion cubs born at Whipsnade Zoo for eleven years*

Homes

Triumphantly, **Harold Macmillan** was able to announce the completion of 319 000 new houses and flats in Britain that year to over-fulfil his target of 300 000 and make his name as a Minister of immense determination. That he had done so by diverting resources from schools and hospitals and by lowering building standards was largely ignored (except by **Nye Bevan,** his opponent in Parliament) and little cared about by those who had until recently been homeless. A new three-bedroomed house might cost £2500, a flat £1500 and the Building Societies' interest rate on loans was 4½ per cent. Building in nearly all the advanced countries was at a high volume to make up for wartime losses and deficiencies. Of the failures, France's was the most ignominious with only 200 000 new houses completed since 1945: there the financial collapse of **Le Corbusier**'s scheme for cheap flats in Marseilles led to their being let at high rents.

In this year **the world's largest building society,** the Halifax, celebrated its centenary. Home **furnishings** of modern and lighter appearance and structure were becoming more common, vigorously stimulated by the ideas of the 1951 Festival of Britain as they caught on in popular form. With this so-called 'contemporary' furniture came an increased use of plastic and a demand for additional space which few European homes could provide but which were becoming far more common in the USA where rooms of irregular shapes were quite normal. In Britain a three-piece bedroom suite could be bought for £70, a double bed for £10 and a 10 ft 6 in square Wilton carpet for £20.

Below: *The Lord Mayor of Birmingham, Ald. W T Bowen, J P, discussing conditions with a slum dweller, as the city's first high rise flats near completion in the background*

Farm transport in India

Food

The state of imbalance in the availability of food in different parts of the world was much the same in 1953 as it is today. The developed countries consumed more than they really needed while many people who lived in under-developed lands were on the verge of starvation. Efforts by the UN Food and Agricultural Organisation to improve matters were hampered by shortage of funds – only a $750 000 increase was made in the annual budget and much of that was spent by experts in holding their various meetings. World food production was rising steadily year by year, and 1953 was good in that there were few major crop failures. However, increases barely kept up with demand (in India, for example, nearly 3 million more had to be fed) though the sharp rise in prices which had distinguished 1951 and 1952 at last diminished.

In Britain, (as recorded on p. 31) the end of rationing was in sight and food prices, stabilised by subsidies, remained very similar to those of 1952. Prices charged in the grocers' shops were as below:

Potatoes	2d (1p) per lb (450 g).
Butter	4s (20p) per lb rationed in June at 4 oz (113 g) per person per week.
Milk	7d (4p) per pint (0.5 l).
Meat	2s (10p) per lb rationed in June at 2s 4d per person per week (and virtually unrationed in August) though returning to the ration in November.
Bacon	4s (20p) per lb rationed at 5 oz (141 g) per person per week.
Pork sausages	2s 6d (12½p) per lb.
Ground rice	1s (5p) per lb.
Tea	2s 6d (12½p) per lb.
Cigarettes	1s 3¼d (6¼p) for ten.

During the year eggs, bacon, sugar and sweets came off the ration for good.

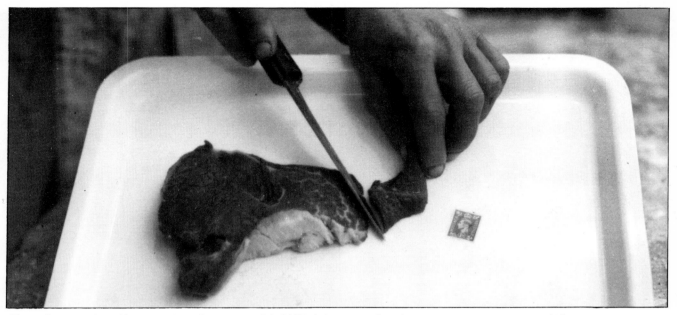

Above: *One person's weekly meat ration in January – worth 1s 9d (7½p), the piece on the right representing a recent increase of 1d*

Annette Mills with 'Muffin the Mule'

The design of **children's toys** was undergoing a process of marked change. Not only was the introduction of plastic materials making the manufacture of toys simpler and cheaper, but it was enabling designers to create products that were far more realistic, a trend eagerly welcomed by children and parents alike. No longer was it enough for a doll's pram or a model railway engine to approximate in shape and colour to the real thing; now it had to be a faithful replica (working if possible) based on one of the latest inventions, such as space rockets and washing machines, that sold well in the shops. Television creations too had a strong influence, reflected in a vigorous demand for soft toys modelled on favourites such as **Muffin the Mule.** The old subjects remained but were being swiftly overwhelmed by a host of modern ideas.

Tri-ang
Regd. Trade Mark

Pedal Motor Car "Thirty" B. For ages 2 to 5½ years. 79 11d.

Tricycle (Model 3 16B). Latest twin-tube frame—with boot. £8 9s. 5d. 36 other models, at popular prices.

Bin Tricycle 910B. Ball-bearing Drive. 52 6d. 10 other popular models.

"Servis" Washing Machine. Really washes doll's clothes. 14" high. Price—Hand 37 6. Electric 56 6.

Fairycycle "OS" with Stabiliser. The ideal "first" cycle for 4-5 year olds. £6 2s. 11d. 5 other models from £5 9s. 10d. to £8 7s. 5d.

Pedigree W Doll—walks, sleeps, flirts, stands. 21" high. 12 other models 9/6 to 91/-.

"Sovereign" Doll's Pram. Replica of famous full size Pedigree model. £10 5s. 0d.

Sheepdog Chassis Toy. Approximately 25" long—handle height 15". 83 6d. 12 other dogs and animals available from 47 3d.

Pedalkar 550. Length 24½ in. Ball-bearing. 45 6d. 9 other models from 17 - to 54 11d.

Teddy Bear. 18 models in various sizes from 12" to 23". Prices from 10 - to 57 6.

"Foxhunter" Rocker. Steel horse with large rubber saddle. Length 43½ in. £5 13s. 9d. 6 other Rocking Horses from 24 6d. to £15 5s. 0d.

Blackboard Easel 110. 47½". Board 24 31/-. 6 other from 9 6d.

Juvenile Cycle. Model 20 P.G. £10 13. 7d. 11 other models for boys and girls from £8 10s. to £13 16s. 5d.

Tri-ang Doll's Pram 20 AMT—a distinctive model. Steel body, washable hood and apron. 69 6d.

Doll's House No. 61. Length 19". 56 11d. 11 other models from 37 6d. to £16 16s. 0d.

Scooter 120. Steel frame. Length 27½". 19 6d. 8 other models from 11 6d. upwards.

The Bride (3 6d.), **Jenny Wren** and **Guardsman** (6 3)—three in the ful series of 37 Pedigree Nursery and Character Dolls. All 7" tall.

Pedigree "Delite" Doll (No. 16SW 2). 16" high. Sleeps, flirts. "Ma Ma" voice. 28 3d. Other models from 2 3d. to £9 10s. 0d.

"Minor" Pedal Tractor for ages 2½ to 5. Length 34". 78 9d. "Major" model £5 19s. 6d.

Mechanical Mixer with lemon squeezer. 9". 16 9d.

Letters and Numbers. Gaily coloured in plastic. 2" high. 30 assorted letters and 10 numbers. 12 6d.

Trotting "Machine". Horse trots realistically. Pedal driven. Length 43". £8 2s. 6d.

Push Horse. No. 130. Seat 14½" long. 29 6. 5 other models from 24 6 to £5 19s. 0d.

Pedigree "Elizabeth" Dressmaking Doll. (No. 19SW E) 19" high. Complete with set of patterns. 42 -.

Pedigree "Beryl" 19" Pin-Up Doll. (No. 19SW.PV). Complete with "Play-Perm" Kit. 47 6d. Many other models.

Tricycle. Model 1016 with BALL-BEARING drive. 45 5s. 0d. 10 other models from 25 11d. upwards.

Doll's Sunkar No. 1. 21½" high. 27 3d. De-luxe model 45 6d.

Pedigree "R Hood" Doll. 7" 8 6d. Many Nursery Rhyme Character Dolls 4 9d.

The world's largest range of toys

oys for us!

Minic Clockwork Sherman Tank No. 2 Climbs, fires sparks and smoke. Length 8¾". 25/-.

Minic Clockwork No. 2 Bulldozer. Tough and powerful. Emits smoke. Length 7¼". 21/-.

Jones KL44 Crane with Grab. Height of cabin 7½". 31/-. 6 other cranes from 9/- to 37/6.

"Penguin" Ocean Racing Yacht. Length 16". Price 26/-. Smaller 10". Racer—price 5/11d.

Minic "Push and Go" No. 2 Fire-fighter. Actually squirts water. Length 8¼". Price 28/3d.

Minic Clockwork -Ton Tipper with ower operated tip ody. Length 7¼". 2/-.

Excavator No. 300. Perfect working model with 7 controls. Cabin height 8¼". 37/6d.

Covered Lorry (No. WS59). Strong metal. Length 9¼". Price 7/3d. Many other similar models from 3/5d.

Fixit Truck — complete with spare wheel, set of tools and lifting jack. 8¼" long. 8/6d.

Minic Clockwork Diesel Road Roller. With gears and brake. Length 7¼". 12/6d.

Rainbow Humming Top. 5" diameter. Hums and changes colour. 4/11d. 9 other models from 2/11 to 15/-.

Minic "Push and Go" "Zephyr" Fire-Chief Car. Length 7". 10/6d.

Tricycle. Model 6/16 P.B. with pneumatic tyred 16" wheels and luggage boot. £13 6s. 10d. Other models from £5 0s. 3d. to £13 11s. 2d.

"Remote Control" Builder's Lorry. (No. 2015). Open tip body. Other similar models 28/3d.

Brick Lorry. (No. 6152). Complete with load of bricks. Length 9¾". 33/3d. Other lorries from 3/3d.

LOCO No. 24. All-metal. Length 21". 21/6d. 5 other models from 16/9 upwards.

ORT "Y." Length ". 18/9d. 9 other dels from 11/3d. 89/3d.

"Try to Spell" Bricks. 36—1¼" cube bricks with rounded corners. 12/11d.

Minic Clockwork Mechanical Horse and Trailer with 6" Cruiser. Length 8¼". 9/-.

"Sixty" Ball-Bearing Pedal Motor Car. For ages 3 to 7 years. £6 13s. 6d. 26 other models from 39/6d. upwards.

Minic Clockwork "Great Spider." A real winner. Length 4½". 4/6d. 17 other novelty models from 2/3d. upwards.

Dog in Mohair. ong. Price 12/3d. her soft toys from to 57/6d.

Bubble Express. Pull-along toy. Emits real bubbles. Length 12". 19/6d.

Steel Barrow No. 100. Length 28½". 18/6d. 6 other models from 9/6 to 28/3d.

"Super Jet" Motor Cycle. Stabilizer on rear wheel. 75/11d.

Tricycle (Model 2/12). Chain drive. £5 8s. 1d. also fitted with a boot £5 18s. 7d.

omething for every boy and girl

Health

Although 1953 was to go down in history as the year in which an effective **vaccine against infantile paralysis** was introduced (see page 30) this was but one small contribution by medical science to the vast changes affecting health patterns and mortality rates. Since 1946 in Britain, for example, **maternal mortality** had fallen by one half and there was a considerable reduction in tuberculosis besides the strong control upon infections effected by **antibiotics,** of which no less than six new kinds were announced during the year. But as a result of increased

A machine for testing the contents of a smoking cigarette. (1) Cigarette, (2) Filter, (3) & (4) Holders, (5) Vacuum valve, (6) Blowing-out tube, (7) Lung

longevity the higher incidence of death from **heart complaints** and **cancer** became all the more plain, notably the cases of lung cancer which were caused, it was assumed, by tobacco smoking and atmospheric pollution. Warned by reports of the high death rate in December 1952 from 'smog', the British took to wearing **'smog masks'** in 1953 and the papers were filled with all sorts of speculation. Research into cancer certainly stole the headlines when it was realised that, in ageing populations, more died from this disease than from tuberculosis. News of work on **artificial hearts** also attracted interest though progress was not very dramatic. The commercial introduction of **radioactive cobalt units** gave promise of more efficient X-Ray treatment than was possible with the existing 'tube' machines.

Animal health also occupied a prominent place in the public's attention, mainly in connection with strenuous efforts in Britain and Holland to eradicate tuberculosis in cattle (as had been achieved in Denmark the previous year) and to deal with brucellosis. With the latter there was transitory success in the USA, but the disease still defies absolute control 25 years later. Sympathetic concern was also expressed for rabbits which were being ravaged by **myxomatosis** in France and Belgium (after the deliberate introduction of the virus near Paris in 1952) and now was detected in Kent. Since all attempts to prevent its spread had failed, the owners of domestic rabbits were extremely alarmed.

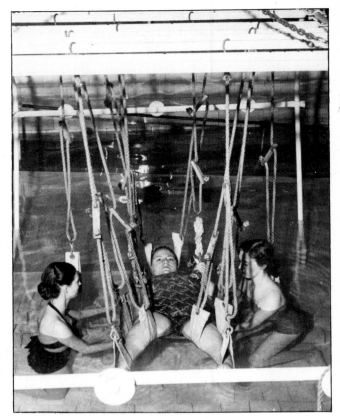

Treatment for a polio victim at Leamington Spa

For human beings, however, this was a normal year, lacking in great epidemics. A better and longer life ahead seemed assured as medical science promised more miracles in the form of new 'wonder' drugs and artificial organs.

Education

Modern primary school classroom in Crawley New Town, Sussex

In the aftermath of the heavy inflation and related economics of 1952, only the smallest improvements in educational standards took place anywhere. Even in the

USA there was overcrowding in schools (one out of five of which were dangerous as fire risks), and the institutions of higher education were $250 million short of their cash needs. Almost everywhere there was a demand for technical education that could not be fulfilled due to a shortage of trained teachers. In Britain, where teachers' salaries, on the Burnham Scale, stood at £415–£670 for men and £370–£536 for women, the most far-reaching proposal of the year (apart from a change in wage scales) was that put forward by the Labour Party to create **'Comprehensive Schools'** and abolish Grammar Schools in the interests of equality. The proposal was rejected at the Party's annual conference, on educational grounds as much as any other, with **Hugh Gaitskell,** the Shadow Chancellor, suggesting that it might be better if more

working class children were placed in public schools. Once more in the USA, where Negroes had the highest rate of illiteracy, the vexed ruling by the Supreme Court on the case of **Brown v Plessey** in connection with segregation of pupils was postponed for further consideration. World-wide, the problem of illiteracy was being slowly overcome, though there were those who worried that the increase in television watching by children might lower reading standards – a threat which has been substantiated since in some areas. The demand for books continued at a high level with Britain exporting a record number to the value of £15 million. The average cost of a book stood at 14s 4d (73p), a level that was easier to maintain since the price of paper and printing had recently fallen and there were new cheaper processes under development.

Religion

In the USA the travelling baptist minister, **Billy Graham,** continued to draw enormous congregations whenever he spoke at his public meetings. His revivalist campaign, run on traditional business lines, was stimulated by the production of his first book, the successful *Peace with God.* In Britain, the year was illuminated by the launching of an appeal by the **Church of England** for £4 million to repair and restore its ancient buildings. A little later various ecclesiastical reforms came under consideration, such as closer links with the so-called Free Churches, a revision of the Canon Law of 1603 and moves to involve the laity more closely with synodal government. Reform was also being undertaken within the Church of Rome by **Pope Pius XII** through his policy of abrogating the custom of maintaining a majority of Italian cardinals by the creation of 24 new cardinals from other nations. And everywhere throughout the world the churches of all faiths endeavoured to combat the inroads made by Communism, using many forms of propaganda available from newspapers, books and radio to television.

Above: *Bill Graham the evangelist, addresses a crowd of 40 000 people from the steps of the Capitol Building, Washington, DC*

Below: *The accused in the trial of the SS perpetrators of the Oradour-sur-Glane massacre. First row:* The Alsations: Graffe, Elsaesser and Hollinger. *Second row:* Ochs, Lohner, Giedinger. *Third row:* Prestel, Weber and Niess

The Law

Although crime in Britain did not exhibit any marked change in incidence (see page 101), legislation was introduced to make it an offence to carry an offensive weapon in public places, and there was renewed debate upon the desirability of abolishing the death penalty. But whereas the **process of law** in Britain was **unattended by celebrated cases,** in France the delayed trial of 21 members of the German SS unit (including 13 Alsatians) which had massacred 642 inhabitants of **Oradour-sur-Glane** in 1944, led to political uproar. Sentences of death or imprisonment on the accused aroused such anger among the populace of Alsace that a special bill was passed through the National Assembly granting them an amnesty – a move which produced a reactionary fury in other parts of France.

In the USA a new Chief Justice, **Earl Warren,** was appointed on the death of **Frederick Vinson.** The Supreme

Court dealt with its usual wide range of cases: from proclaiming baseball a sport to several important examples affecting Civil Rights, often of a racial or religious nature; denying **Alger Hiss** a retrial of his case for perjury connected with espionage; and rejecting last minute pleas by the atom spies, **Julius and Ethel Rosenberg,** against sentences of death – which were carried out on 19 June.

Cases of **International Law** were many and usually of political hue, associated in some instances with the ownership of **Persian oil.** The case of the tanker *Rose Mary* was decided in Britain's favour in January by the Aden supreme court but another in respect of Persian oil carried by the *Miriella* was adverse in a lower Italian court. The treatment of **prisoners of war** by the North Koreans and attempts by the USA to establish an international criminal court were also considered. Before the **International Court,** Italy brought charges against her previous enemies, France, Britain and the USA, in respect of gold removed during the war in 1943 from Rome.

Fuel

A conservative estimate in 1953 judged that only 25 years supply of oil at current rates of consumption from known sources remained. In consequence the search for new sources went on unabated and thus, of particular interest, was the culmination of a 16 year struggle in the US courts regarding offshore 'rights'. During a prolonged debate in Congress, **Senator Wayne Morse** delivered himself of **the longest ever uninterrupted filibuster** of 22 hours 26 minutes on 24/25 April, prior to a bill being passed giving the States rights to all inland waters out to 3 miles (4.8 km) (with certain exceptions) while retaining full rights to the federal authority out to and beyond 200 miles. (320 km). It was signed by the President on 22 May, thus establishing the ownership of unimagined millions of tons of oil and natural gas besides fishing rights and other mineral wealth – this in a year when, at Bakersfield, California, **the record for deep drilling** was beaten at 21 482 ft (6547 metres).

Senator Wayne Morse of Oregon

For the purposes of most industrialised nations, however, coal continued to be the main source of heat and power, though in the USA production had fallen by 5 million to 453 million tons, and in Britain by 3 million to 227 million tons allied to a decline in quality and a rise in price (the British householder was paying about £6 per ton). In West Germany production was up 1 million tons at 124 million, and in the USSR 318 million tons were mined, an increase of 17 million. Electricity, as a clean fuel, was more popular than ever, and cheap too – in Britain it was about 1¼d (1p) per unit and cheaper still in those countries such as Switzerland and the USA with a surplus of hydro-generating capacity. There were no serious shortages, strikes were few and far between in the industries affected, so those with money did not go cold.

Money

Despite the customary gloomy reports that the recession of 1952 was far from over, business began to boom as inflation came under control and the money supply became easier in the industrialised countries. In July **Germany,** moving into the lead in European trade, had a surplus of DM600 million while Britain, whose Conservative Government was steadily dismantling price controls and containing wage demands, recouped much of what she had lost in 1952, and ended up with a surplus of £170 million on the year with the **bank rate** down in September from 4 to 3½ per cent. As for the **Stock Exchanges,** New York, which started the year at 263 on the Standard and Poor Index, moved narrowly and finished lower at 254, while the London market rose from 119 on the *Financial Times* index in January to 130 at the end of the year. **General Motors** of the USA, showing tangibly how good it was for America, reported record sales for 1953 at $10 027 985 482 with 44.8 per cent of the market for passenger cars. The biggest private corporation of all turned out to be **Metropolitan Life Insurance Co** of the USA with assets at $12 312 million. On the London Stock Exchange the main topic of the year was provided by a new activity, the take-over bid. Early in the year **Charles Clore** made a

Charles Clore, the financier at St. Moritz

A casino set up on board a moored vessel – quite legal in Britain as the boats drop anchor outside the 3-mile limit where no gambling laws apply.

Street betting – quite illegal in Britain

£4 million bid for J Sears & Co (The True Form Boot Co) exploiting the undervaluation of the victim for a cheap purchase. Similar bids, followed by others, particularly for stores, resulted in speculation and rumours becoming rife and the threatened companies feeling compelled to take protective measures by raising their dividends and adjusting their policies. It was nothing if not stimulating and caused the authorities to examine the probity of such activity and later to establish new rules in such matters.

Savings tended to fall with massive withdrawals of £66 million in Britain from the Post Office Savings Bank, which still paid interest at a traditionally low 2 per cent. On the other hand the **Cost of Living** in the countries given below showed a far less volatile situation than that for the previous two years:

	Sept 1953	Sept 1952
Britain	130	126
USA	115	114
Germany	107	109
France	141	146
Australia	179	173
Canada	121	110
South Africa	137	129

Gambling in Britain declined marginally, as it had in 1952, though there was an increase of £6 million to £70 million in the money invested in **Football Pools,** whose top prize was £75000. **Lotteries** were rejected by the legislature in the USA but gambling there continued to increase, much of it illegally conducted bingo on the sidewalks. In other countries the trend moved slightly upward as the end of the recession came in sight. Lotteries were a way of life in France, a system to which the people of New Jersey State in the USA moved closer when, in November, they voted to make raffles legal for the benefit of churches.

Politics
in France and Western Germany

Among the more sophisticated countries, **France** provided a permanent source of interest to the educated people of the world by the manifestations of instability in her Governments. Hardly a month passed without some kind of crisis developing. **René Mayer** became prime minister on 7 January, lasting until 23 May when he was defeated over his inability to solve the budget crisis and

Above: *Dr Konrad Adenauer electioneering in Cologne*

Below: *Rev Chad Varah – a self-styled human fire-watcher*

obtain special powers. There then ensued the longest interregnum in French parliamentary history when no less than four candidates failed to form a government. Finally a solution was reached on 26 June when **Joseph Laniel** took office. He managed only to keep his head above water, was plagued by strikes, harried by the deteriorating situation in Indo-China (see pages 12–13), and at the end of the year was locked in traditional controversy over the next budget.

In **Western Germany,** on the other hand, the victory by **Konrad Adenauer's** Christian Democratic Party, with 45 per cent of the poll, gave him, as Chancellor, the opportunity to govern through an alliance with the Refugee and the Free Democratic and German parties. Affecting many Europeans, besides Germans, was the problem of reconciling the emotional desire to reunify Germany with that of joining the **EDC** which had been signed as a treaty in 1952 (with the implication of re-establishing German armed forces) but which had still to be ratified by France where a bill had yet to be brought before the Assembly.

At the end of the year there was a feeling of rising hope, buoyed up in many countries as a conviction that everyday life was improving in quality and that the aftermath of the Second World War was over. At the same time the **Reverend Chad Varah** in London, alarmed by a case of suicide, decided in November to launch an organi-sation called **The Samaritans,** designed to dissuade people in distress from taking this course of action.

SECTION 3

THE WORLD OF MACHINES

Ships

The year was notable more for those occasions when a great number of ships were gathered together, rather than for the appearance of any one remarkable vessel. Indeed the largest liner to come into service, the British built Greek liner *Olympia,* weighed but 23 000 tons. **The Coronation Review** at Spithead in June (see page 29) not unnaturally was the outstanding maritime event of the year, but NATO **Exercise 'Mariner',** held in September, attracted the largest number of vessels, some 300 together with 1000 aircraft and 500 000 men. Designed to practise naval forces in the defence of the Western Approaches to Europe, the navies of nine nations were involved for 19 days, during the course of which the British cruiser *Swiftsure* collided with the destroyer *Diamond.* **The most dramatic voyage of the year** was that undertaken by the British submarine *Andrew* which, in 15 days, completed **the first totally submerged crossing of the Atlantic** using a new type of 'snort' tube for breathing.

Above: *The crew of HM Submarine* Andrew *home after their record breaking 3200 mile (5150 km) submerged Atlantic crossing*

Below: *Scene during a naval exercise in the eastern Mediterranean*

At this time **the largest fleet in the world** belonged to the USA with 15 battleships, 101 aircraft carriers and 75 cruisers – considerably more than the 5 battleships, 18 aircraft carriers and 25 cruisers of the Royal Navy, and significantly ahead of the Soviet fleet with its 3 battleships and 20 cruisers. **The mercantile marine** of the USA was also larger than that of Britain – 25 million to 19 million tons, with Norway third largest in the world at 6 million tons.

Of the new ships coming into service the most important change was in the size of **oil tankers.** The largest at sea in January was about 30 000 tons, but the Japanese had produced some of 38 000 tons and the Germans built a 45 700 tonner, the *Tina Onassis*, a type of ship that was already recognised as a serious risk by way of pollution of the sea.

Shipbuilding, world wide, maintained the production of previous years with emphasis on tanker construction even though demand for these ships was temporarily down owing to fewer cargoes. In June by far **the greatest ship building nation** was Britain, with 2 123 565 tons under construction, compared with 558 000 tons in the USA, and 545 000 tons in Germany, with Japan building only 335 000 tons. Towards the end of the year, however, the Germans moved into second place.

Notable ships nearing completion in Britain were the 30 000 ton liner *Arcadia* and the 43 000 ton aircraft carrier *Ark Royal*, while in the USA work started on **the second nuclear submarine** as well as the 60 000 ton aircraft carriers *Forrestal* and *Saratoga*.

Launch of the world's biggest oil tanker, the 45 720 ton Tina Onassis. *Tankers more than ten times the size have been launched 25 years later*

Aircraft and Rockets

The public was treated to a succession of speed record bids as rival firms competed for orders for the latest jet aircraft. **On no less than five occasions the absolute speed record was broken:**

				mph	km/h
16 July	Lt-Col William Barns	USA	North American F86D	715.75	1151.89
7 Sep	Sqn Ldr Neville Duke	GB	Hawker Hunter 3	727.63	1171
15 Sep	Lt-Cmdr Michael Lithgow	GB	Supermarine Swift 4	735.70	1183.99
3 Oct	Lt-Cmdr James Verdin	USA	Douglas F4D-1	752.94	1211.74
29 Oct	Lt-Col Frank Everest	USA	North American F100A	755.15	1215.30

Sqn-Ldr Neville Duke pilots the Hawker Hunter *to the world's air speed record. He flew the sleek aircraft at an average speed of 727.6 mph (1171 km/h)*

And on 18 May **Jacqueline Cochrane** (USA) in an F86 became **the first woman to break the sound barrier.**

Speed records over long distances were dominated by **English Electric Canberra** light bombers. Five of these machines were the sole entrants in the speed section of the London to Christchurch (NZ) air race on 8 October, the winner of which completed the course in 23 h 52 min (494.4 mph (796 km/h)) with four refuelling stops. The transport section was won on handicap by a piston-engined **Douglas DC-6A** of KLM in 49 h 57 min, but the fastest time for an airliner was clocked by the **Vickers Viscount** in 40 h. Records by the **Canberra** (the aircraft which flew the Coronation TV film to Canada) were numerous:

27/28 Jan	London to Port Darwin	average speed 391.2 mph (630 km/h)	22 h
17 Dec	London to Cape Town	average speed 486.6 mph (783 km/h)	12 h 21 min
19 Dec	Cape Town to London	average speed 452.8 mph (729 km/h)	13 h 6 min

The Canberra bomber back from New Zealand with pilot Flt-Lt R Burton and navigator Flt-Lt D Gannon. Their flying time from London to Christchurch was 23 h 52 min

Below: The world's largest transport helicopter the Piasecki YH-16 at Philadelphia International Airport. With an overall length of 134 ft (40.8m), this transporter could carry 40 troops, 32 stretcher patients, or three jeeps

Absolute human altitude and speed records were both improved by Americans in 1953. The altitude record of 83 235 ft (25 370 m) was set by Lt-Col Marion E Carl in a Douglas D558-II **Skyrocket** on 21 August and the speed record of 1612 mph (2594 km/h) by Major Charles Elwood Yeager in a Bell X-1A on 12 December.

World speed and altitude records for helicopters were also captured by a **Piasecki YN-21** in the USA with a top speed of 146.1 mph (235 km/h) and a height of 22 500 ft (6858 m).

In the commercial world a great debate took place over the competitive effectiveness of prop jet and pure jet airliners, as represented, respectively, by the **British Vickers Viscount** and **DH Comet.** Already it had been shown that the prop jet engine was superior to piston types; the question was whether or not the pure jet could overcome the disadvantages of the Comet, the Mark I version of which carried only 36 passengers and was only marginally profitable, even though it was much faster than any other airliner in the world over medium distances. A Comet I, for example, flew from London to Tokyo and back (20 400 miles (32 630 km)) in 74 h 52 min on 3–7 April, with several refuelling stops. The Mark 2 version flew in August and work on it was in progress for 50 orders. In fact, the airlines were convinced already that the future must lie with the big pure jet. In Britain **Vickers** were projecting a crescent winged transport capable of flying the Atlantic at 600 mph (965 km/h) with 100 passengers, and in the USA **Boeing** were beginning work on the design of what was to be one of the most successful of all jet air liners – the **707.** Air transport, so important in a country as large as the USA, took revolutionary steps forward there. **The first daily nonstop coast to coast route** (8 h travel) was inaugurated by TWA with Super Constellation air liners; **a helicopter service** linking the New York airports of La Guardia and Newark was begun, and financial concessions were made to stimulate the carriage of mail and freight.

Fewer important new aircraft appeared than in 1952, which had been a bumper year; these included:

Britain: The **Folland Gnat,** a very small cheap fighter
Canada: The twin engined, 14 seat **DH Otter**
USA: The **Piasecki YH-16,** the world's largest helicopter with the capacity to lift 40 soldiers.

After the intense interest generated in 1952 about **space projects,** confident forecasts were made in 1953, notably by **Dr Werner von Braun** who had made Germany's V2 rockets in the war. He prophesied **manned orbiting satellites** within 10 or 15 years, while US scientists talked of rockets equipped with radar for the location of enemy surface targets. Meanwhile in the USA, Britain and USSR the development of all manner of rocket motors became increasingly important and the USA fired its first **Redstone** ballistic, medium range, surface to surface missile.

Railways

Under pressure from the competition of road transport (which, in Britain, in May, was largely freed from public ownership by the latest Transport Act) railways everywhere endeavoured to rationalise their methods, lower their costs and speed up transit. Steam was rapidly being replaced by diesel and electric propulsion, particularly in the USA and on the Continent, though much more slowly in Britain. In Germany they were developing freight wagons to carry two tiers of motor cars. **A world record for speed on rails** was achieved in France by the **Co-Co electric locomotive No. 7121** drawing three coaches at an average speed of 150.9 mph (242.9 km/h) over 3 miles. In that country, however, fares went up by 25 per cent whereas other nations were managing to contain such increases to a much lower level, though deficits were incurred as a result.

Railway construction was particularly active in Canada, whereas in the USA the pace at which lines were being abandoned was accelerating. In South Australia conversion was completed to a broad gauge line. In Britain though there was little change in length of track in service; there it was hoped that a new machine might eliminate the need for a man with a hammer to tap wheels to see if they were cracked.

The French locomotive Co-Co at record breaking speed

Road Transport

The year marked a turning point for the motor car industry in that, for the first time since the war, sufficient vehicles were being produced to generate enough competition between makers to persuade them to cut their prices. In terms of car production the principal manufacturing nations were as follows:

USA	6 116 948	Top manufacturer: General Motors
Britain	570 000	40% exported with 25% of European market. Top manufacturer: British Motor Corporation
France	475 000	Top manufacturer: Renault
West Germany	470 000	with 39% of the European market. Top manufacturer: Volkswagen
Italy	131 000	Top manufacturer: Fiat.

Above: *The cheaper end of the road passenger transport market. Douglas 'Vespa' 125 cc £120 16s 8d. 120 mpg at 35 mph. 'Winged Wheel' 35 cc approx £25 200 mpg. BSA 'Bantam' 123 cc £87 12s 0d. 179 mpg at 30 mph. Bond 'Minicar' 197 cc £275. 85 mpg. at 45 mph. Austin A30 two-door 8 hp £475 14s 2d. 50 mpg at 30 mph. Standard 8 8 hp £481 7s 6d. 55 mpg at 30 mph. Morris Minor II 8 hp £529 10s 10d. 41 mpg at 50 mph. Volkswagen 10 hp £649 19s 2d. 38 mpg.*

Moves were afoot to establish a Japanese motor industry using British and German components and expertise, but these did not progress very fast. Britain remained the dominant producer of **motor cycles,** manufacturing 155 000 and exporting over 6000 to the USA. But production of **pedal cycles** was down by 1 million compared with 1952, mainly due to a fall in export orders. A low priced machine in Britain cost about £10.

Petrol in Britain cost 4s 3d (21p) per gallon (4.5 l) (and, from February, was sold under **brand names for the first time since the war**) and the flat rate road tax for cars was £12 10s (£12.50) per annum. Taxes were sufficiently low to encourage more people to own cars: the number of new registrations that year rose by 70 000 to 260 000 and the cost of the cheapest family car was £400.

Innovations of the year
- **The first production car with a 'wrap round' windscreen** appeared in the USA.
- **The first successful radial-ply tyre** was produced by Michelin.
- **The first series production car with a glass fibre body** was produced by Chevrolet.
- **The first transposed number plates** (with numbers before letters) appeared in Britain.

Below: *The return of branded petrol to Britain, but attendants with skates were only an ephemeral gimmick*

Farewell of the year

The highly successful British Jaguar XK120 was taken out of production, 92 per cent of its production having been exported in five years.

In **Motor Sport** the greatest fame rested upon the Italian driver **Alberto Ascari.** By winning the Belgian and Dutch Grand Prix at the start of the season he established **an unbeaten world record of eight consecutive GP wins,** all in Ferrari cars, and that year went on to win the world championship once more. He was hardly troubled by **Juan Fangio,** though threatened at times by the rising star of British motor racing, **Mike Hawthorn,** who was also driving for Ferrari. Of the other great road racing or touring events of the year the following were the winners:

			mph	km/h
Le Mans 24 h race	**Tony Rolt** and **Duncan Hamilton**	Jaguar	105.85	170
Indianapolis 500 mile race	**Billy Yuzkovich**	Fuel Injection Special	128.74	207
Mille Miglia	**Giannino Marzotto**	Ferrari	142.34	229

Above: Hon Sally Noel Buxton at the wheel of a Jaguar XK 120 (3442 cc) during the Brighton Speed Trials

Below: Mike Hawthorn (Ferrari) leads Giuseppe Farina (Ferrari) during the German Grand Prix at Nuerburgring in August. Farina won

In **Rallying,** for the second year running, a British car (Ford Zephyr) driven by **Maurice Gastonides** won the Monte Carlo Rally while **Mr and Mrs Ian Appleyard** won their fourth successive Coupe des Alpes (with an unpenalised run), he to become the first of two recipients of the coveted Coupe d'Or for three successive victories. In the USA the National Automobile Champion was **Sam Hanks.** And in East Africa they ran a special **'East African Coronation Safari' Rally,** an event which was already extremely exacting (with classes determined by car price in East Africa rather than engine capacity) and which has since evolved into the toughest rally in the calendar.

In **Motor Cycle racing** the struggle for supremacy between Italian and British machines was intense. Respectively, in the 125 and 250 cc classes, an **MV-Agusta** and a **Moto-Guzzi,** won at the Isle of Man TT races, but **Nor-**

Geoff Duke on a Gilera during the TT Race in the Isle of Man

tons took the 350 and 500 cc events and nearly all the honours in Australia, New Zealand and South Africa. The top celebrities were Britain's **Dick Amm** and **Les Graham,** though Graham was killed shortly after winning the 125 cc event at the Isle of Man.

The ACE – one of the most complicated pieces of machinery ever built and the most versatile computer of its kind in the world

The Road Racing World Champions were:

125 cc	Werner Haas	West Germany on an NSU
250 cc	Werner Haas	West Germany on an NSU
350 cc	Fergus Anderson	Britain on a Moto-Guzzi
500 cc	Geoff Duke	Britain on a Gilera 4
Sidecar	Eric Oliver	Britain on a Norton.

Road racing World Championship, winning companies:

125 cc solo	MV-Agusta	Italy
250 cc solo	NSU	Germany
350 cc solo	Moto-Guzzi	Italy
500 cc solo	Gilera	Italy
500 cc sidecar	Norton	Britain

In the USA, where motor cycling was among the less popular sports, **Pete Goldsmith** won the US Championship at Daytona Beach on a **Harley-Davidson.**

Highways under construction multiplied, the USA taking a long lead in the building of four-lane divided highways to cope with the colossal increase in traffic density. Toll highways, of which only 734 miles (1181 km) were in use that year, were gaining in popularity, but most expenditure went on improvements to existing roads. In Europe, with the exception of Britain where there was a marked reluctance to spend much money on road improvement at all, the emphasis was also on improvements rather than new construction. Ambitious plans for motorways were being laid in Italy, France and Germany, though in the case of the latter's **Autobahnen** it was noted with alarm that the long stretches built before the war were beginning to break up under the weight of modern traffic.

Electronics, Mechanisation and Machine Tools

The most practical innovation when related to **computers,** was the installation of **the first memory store computers** in the USA, an innovation that was to revolutionise all manner of scientific and managerial techniques over the years to come. Though still in their infancy, computers were beginning to make an impact in a number of fields. In Britain there were ten in use and ten under development; in the USA 15 in use and 150 under development, a clear indication that the Americans were investing more money than the British or any other nation. Already computers were in use for calculation and soon their analytical capacity would be employed for high speed working. **Oracle,** an American computer built in 1953, could memorise up to 4 million words, it was claimed, and now a problem arose, in developing tape machines and automatic typewriters that could print out the outflow of information at a fast enough speed. Another revolutionary announcement was that by the

US Signal Corps describing **printed circuits** that made it possible drastically to simplify otherwise complex wiring arrangements. Only later would it be found that they also dramatically improved reliability.

Among the large number of areas in which electronics were employed was that of **weather forecasting.** Radar was developed that could detect an oncoming storm and give precise warning of its outbreak – as was demonstrated in New York in July. Also in the USA it was announced that talk of long-range weather forecasting aided by computers would be converted into reality in 1954.

Machine tools of the most modern kind, notably those of the 'transfer' type that could link several processes by conveyors, were in high demand in the USA where the greatest number of automatic and semi-automatic machines were being installed, mainly to help implement the immense rearmament programme.

Heavy Engineering and Power Supply

The major heavy engineering projects of the post war years, apart from shipbuilding (see page 48), were those related to electric power supply. Leeway, caused by the war-time standstill, had to be made up and headway made to cater for vastly increased demand. Hydroelectric projects were much in the news; in Russia the completion of **the VI Lenin dam** (Kuibyshev) enclosed a lake of 13.68 miles² (57 km²), the **largest in the world at that time,** and in Canada, where a huge programme of farm electrification was 75 per cent complete, two tunnels of 10.1 miles (16.2 km) were finished at **Kemano** for a hydro-electric project. Hydro projects were usually related in some way to agriculture and often to flood control: **the Missouri river flood control and irrigation schemes** were being devised with a budget of $91 million and would include four big dams; in India the 7942 ft (2420 m) **Tungabhadra dam,** part of a large power and irrigation system in the south, was nearing completion.

At work on the Lenin dam at Kuibyshev on the Volga

Most of the **bridges** which had been destroyed during the war had been replaced and now there were many ambitious projects in all countries to build motorway bridges over wide gaps that had hitherto been beyond engineering feasibility, (see also page 65).

Among **the heavier machine tools,** weighing 800 tons, was an aluminium forging press at Redditch, Worcestershire, which could exert a pressure of 12 000 tons and, of particularly ingenious design, a 2500 ton press in the USA, which squeezed out steel tubes using molten glass as a lubricant for the hot metal billets.

Handling devices at the atomic pile, Oak Ridge, Tenn., USA

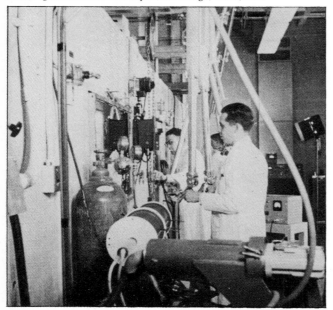

Looking well into the future were those scientists and engineers committed to nuclear projects; not just the schemes geared to weapon production, but the Americans, British, Canadians, French and Soviets who were trying to convert reactors into sources of power. At Oak Ridge in the USA a **nuclear reactor** was operated at full power to generate 150 kW of electricity, and there too the nuclear engine of the first atomic submarine, *Nautilus*, was tested. In Britain, at Harwell, studies were in progress on a **small breeder reactor,** and plans to build **the Calder Hall power station** were announced.

Weapons

Overriding every other consideration in weapon development were the awesome advances made in the nuclear field (see page 26). At the same time several armies found themselves compelled to fight local wars employing obsolete weapons. So, while the USA successfully fired its first atomic shell from the 280 mm cannon on 25 May and exploded eleven other devices that year, the British detonated one atomic bomb and several more were set off by the Soviets. Meanwhile, the vast majority of weapons in the hands of fighting men were those of 1945 vintage, though the list of weapons coming into service or under development was formidable. For example:

Britain: The **Saracen** six-wheeled armoured personnel carrier.

An aerial bomb which could be steered by reference to a television eye in the nose.

France: A 12-ton eight-wheeled armoured car (EBR) with a 75 mm gun.

USA: The **Redstone** surface to surface ballistic missile. The **Nike** ground to air missile.

The use of **TV** for the first time in scanning troop movements.

Throughout the year comparative tests were carried out in an effort to decide upon a standardised NATO rifle round. Chief contenders were the **Belgian FN rifle** (.28 in. calibre), the British **EM2** and the American **Springfield.** At the end of the year the American .300 in. calibre round was accepted, the British opting to take the Belgian rifle modified to accept the .300 round. At the same time the British went ahead with work on a new 9 mm submachine gun, the Patchet.

The extent to which aircraft could enhance the power of land forces was demonstrated by the US Army and Air Forces when a **Globemaster C 124** transport parachute dropped a record load of 40 000 lb (18 144 kg), and nine C 124s delivered 1008 equipped parachutists in what was described as the **'biggest airdrop by the smallest number of planes in history'.** At about the same time plans were in hand to create a new type of US division carried into battle by 2200 helicopters.

Above: *Testing the quality of milk*

Milk distribution in Edinburgh – old style

Agriculture

The rate of mechanisation of farms which had grown rapidly over the preceding years showed no sign of decelerating as determined efforts were made to put more machinery into the developing countries as well as to reduce costs everywhere by cutting down on labour. This year, as in most others, more complicated machines intended to make it easier to crop such vegetables as potatoes and peas, were displayed at Agricultural Shows. At the same time the collection of produce was being made easier; in Britain, for example, the Scottish Milk Marketing Board introduced as an experiment, **the bulk collection of milk in tankers** instead of in churns.

Research into **the industrialised production of foodstuffs** was becoming much more sophisticated. The American Carnegie Institution and the British Imperial Chemical Industries announced the results of their joint studies into the feasibility of producing enormous quantities of fats and protein from the unicellular alga called **Chlorella.** This, it was suggested, would demand a large engineering project (at present only a pilot plant existed) that might yield 40 tons of dry food per acre per year as compared with one twentieth of that quantity for wheat. So far, however, this project of 1953 has not been translated into practice since operating costs have proved prohibitive.

The next 2000 years in Engineering

Lord Dudley Gordon, President of the Engineering Section of the British Association, gave an address in which he foretold the following future developments:

- **That gravity** might be used as a direct source of power.
- **That uranium** would be used up within 2000 years.
- **That tidal power** would be developed but that this might slow down the Earth's rotation and attract the Moon towards the Earth.
- **That iron and steel** would be essential for hundreds of years (he was himself Chairman of the Sheffield steel firm of Hadfields Ltd).
- **That immense quantities of magnesium** were available to be extracted from below the sea, but that development must start soon otherwise life on the planet might deteriorate within the next 50 to 100 years.

SECTION 4

THE ENTERTAINMENT BUSINESS

Theatre

By one of those strange ironies, the London theatre, eager to put on a show worthy of the occasion by opening (at the Queen's wish) during the Coronation, found itself playing to empty houses. So intent were the enormous crowds on seeing the town that they either stayed away or blocked the streets so effectively that those with tickets could not reach the theatres. Things looked up later and audiences were able to enjoy a year that was renowned more for the quality of actors and productions than for the plays themselves. The only play of note which has been revived many times since was **T S Elliot**'s *The Confidential Clerk*. Opening at the Edinburgh Festival in August and transferring to London in September, it made a hit with critics and audiences alike.

Of the other notable stage productions the following attracted strong attention (see page opposite):

Denholm Elliott and Margaret Leighton in T S Elliot's The Confidential Clerk

Title	Author	Country in which shown	Remarks
The White Carnation	**R C Sherriff**	Britain	Good reception with **Sir Ralph Richardson**
Carrington, VC	**Dorothy and Campbell Christie**	Britain	Success with **Alec Clunes** and **Jenny Laird**
The Living Room	**Graham Greene**	Britain	Success with **Eric Portman** and **Dorothy Tutin**
The Devil's General	**Carl Zuckmayer**	Germany and Britain	Success in Germany, failure in Britain despite **Trevor Howard**'s performance
Paint your Wagon	**Frederick Loewe**	USA and Britain	Success with **Bobby Howes**
Guys and Dolls	**Frank Loesser**	USA and Britain	Great success in Britain with **Lizbeth Webb**
The King and I	**Richard Rodgers** and **Oscar Hammerstein**	USA and Britain	Great success with **Yul Brynner** in USA
The Sleeping Prince	**Terence Rattigan**	Britain	Success with **Laurence Olivier** and **Vivien Leigh**
Can-Can	**Cole Porter** and **Abe Burrows**	USA	Success with **Peter Cookson**
Kismet	**Robert Wright** and **George Forrest**	USA	Success with **Alfred Drake**
Victor Borge's Show		USA	*Tour de force*
The Crucible	**Arthur Miller**	USA	Failure
Camino Real	**Tennessee Williams**	USA	Failure

Theatres around the world mostly had a good year, despite the usual problems of rising costs and unenthusiastic critics. The impact of television had yet to harm them severely since the existing and discriminating theatre audiences much preferred a well produced, live show to the then less sophisticated offerings of television that were already making severe inroads into cinema attendances.

Dora Newton, Vivien Leigh, Laurence Olivier and Martita Hunt in The Sleeping Prince

Cinema

The fierce competition between cinema and television pushed the film companies a step further into extremes of presentation. Having proved in 1952, as they thought, that extravagant films with a high colour content would pull the audiences back from the TV screen, the film tycoons turned to 'gimmicks' as a further means of attracting audiences which nevertheless remained at about 46 million per week in the USA – the same level as in the previous year. Activity centred chiefly upon **three dimensional** presentations that were both simpler and cheaper than the **Cinerama** kind first shown in 1952. First to appear was the system using polaroid spectacles which had been first exhibited in 1939. *Bwana Devil*, a cheap documentary by **Arch Obler,** was the first of such films (in March in the USA). Other companies rapidly followed but found themselves totally out-classed when, in October, **Twentieth Century-Fox** came out with the first full length film, *The Robe,* in **Cinemascope** (a widescreen system using anamorphic lenses which made viewing natural, without spectacles – a process that had first been demonstrated by **Henri Chrétien** in France in 1928).

To a year made sensational by the 'battle of the wide screens', the one in which the 19-year-old **Brigitte Bardot** was 'discovered' at the Cannes Film Festival, and in which **Kenneth More** appeared with **Kay Kendall** and a **1905 Spyker car** in the immortal *Genevieve*, it has to be

Above: *A night out at the cinema for the White family, arriving at the Majestic Cinema, Stoke-on-Trent. Note the prices*

Above: *Not the Mafia but prominent members of the film industry including Sir Michael Balcon* (centre back row) *watching a private showing of* Bwana Devil *through polaroid spectacles*

Below: Genevieve *at rest, with Dinah Sheridan* (left) *and Kay Kendall waiting patiently while Kenneth More and John Gregson* (right) *try to put life back into her*

Trevor Howard and Maria Schell in The Heart of the Matter

Marilyn Monroe and Jane Russell in Gentlemen prefer Blondes

added that two colour films of the Coronation and the one showing the conquest of Everest (filmed by **Tom Stobart**) were among the greatest attractions, worldwide. **The 1953 film that was to win the most Oscars** (eight including that of **best film** and with **the best director, Fred Zinnemann**) was *From Here to Eternity* which, at the time of release, did not rate very highly in the critics' choice – some of whom placed it on a par with *Gentlemen Prefer Blondes*, with **Marilyn Monroe** and **Jane Russell** which failed to achieve honours. For British audiences, and others over the years, **Alec Guinness** in the *Captain's Table* and **Stanley Holloway** in *The Titfield Thunderbolt* (about a locomotive) were much less traumatic than **Jack Hawkins** in *The Cruel Sea* (about the Battle of the Atlan-

tic), or a host of Russians making war in the main importation from that country, *The Battle of Stalingrad*.

As for documentaries, the **Disney Studios** won all the Oscars with *The Living Desert* and *The Alaskan Eskimo*, but one of the best documentaries of the year, *The War at Sea*, was produced for the NBC TV network – another clear indication that the cinema industry, already plagued by the astronomic cost of making 'spectaculars', had to look elsewhere for income and adopt the philosophy, 'if you can't beat 'em, join 'em'. After all, the cinema-goer did not pay that much for his seat – on average in Britain only 1s 9d (9p) – and commercial television in the USA cost the viewer only the price of a set plus the electric power.

Television

The Beverley Sisters

On Coronation Day for **the first time in British TV history more people were watching television than were listening to sound broadcasting** (23 million against 12 million). There were also the millions in the USA and Canada who saw telerecordings as soon as they could be flown across the Atlantic (see also page 49). Technologically it was the year in which the problem of making a set that was capable of resolving both colour and black and white transmissions was solved in the USA. There, the number of stations had risen from 168 in 1952 to 534, and the number of sets in use was estimated at 27 159 511 – with advertising revenue at about $300 million a year. In Britain – where a television licence cost £2, a total of 2 203 345 were issued – more than double the number of the previous year, augmented by a rush to install sets in order to watch the Coronation. In Europe, Germany had most transmitters and sets, the French were making a slow start and the first transmitters in Belgium and Switzerland were opened in November.

A typical British programme, that for a week-day, 30 November, was as follows:

3.15 pm	Newsreel
3.45 pm	Film *Capacity Smith*
5.00 pm	Children's TV
5.30 pm	Shut Down
7.25 pm	Weather Chart
7.30 pm	Newsreel
7.45 pm	Teleclub
8.45 pm	*Round the World in 80 days* (film, though not, of course, the celebrated version of 1956)
9.30 pm	Press Conference
10.00 pm	Three Smart Girls in View – The Beverley Sisters
10.30 pm	News (sound only)

Saturday, 1 December was little different and did not include sport.

This cosy routine was liable to sharp reconsideration, however, if the Government's proposals to set up **Commercial TV,** and thus break the BBC monopoly, were put into operation.

Other notable TV events included:

- Transmissions of **opera** from the Metropolitan in New York.
- The enthusiastic reception of **educational TV** in the USA.
- **First link up between Canada and the USA** in January.
- **First programmes in Japan and Czechoslovakia.**

The cost of a 15 inch tubed monochrome set in Britain was about £90 – relatively more expensive than a colour set 25 years later.

The Goons – Spike Milligan, Peter Sellers and Harry Secombe

Radio Broadcasting

Despite the events of the year showing that television in the USA and Britain was on the point of overtaking radio broadcasting in popular support, there was nothing to suggest that radio would become otiose. It was merely forced to adjust itself to a complementary and perhaps subsidiary role. The number of radio receivers manufactured in the USA was 8 932 638 compared with 6 558 303 in 1952. In Britain reception would be improved by a law brought in to compel new motor cars to have suppressors fitted. People were showing signs of turning more to radio for music and preferring to watch plays, panel games and sport (even though football and baseball promoters resisted it) on television. Nevertheless, in Britain the *Goon Show* with **Peter Sellers, Harry Secombe and Spike Milligan** attracted record audiences, as did *Take it from Here,* whose script writers, **Frank Muir** and **Denis Norden,** were perhaps the best in the business. Educational programmes were assuming a much larger importance with 25 691 schools employing this method in Britain alone.

It was radio broadcasting, of course, which still possessed the greatest world-wide influence. Few countries had television but more and more were acquiring radio broadcasting facilities. Receivers were cheaper than television in the ratio 1 to 5, as reliable miniature models using transistors came into use. The ether was filled with propaganda programmes and newscasts from both sides of the Iron Curtain. Throughout the developing countries, transmitters and receivers were being installed at a high rate. As the wavebands became ever more crowded with the interference of one station by another (quite apart from deliberate jamming by Iron Curtain countries of programmes directed at them from the West), the demand for **Very High Frequency** transmissions became

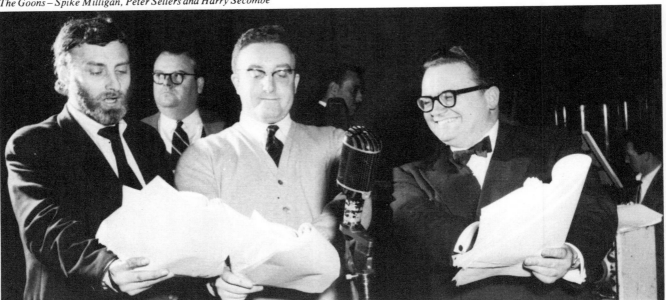

strong. Germany led in this field with 90 such stations; in Britain the BBC stated its need for VHF but reported a revenue deficit of £1.5 million that was delaying such developments.

Music

Though the newspapers and radio gave little critical coverage to **'popular music'**, it had to be recognised that the very term meant simply that more people listened to, or made, that type of tune than bothered with the classics. In the year that in the USA, saw the beginning of **'Rock 'n Roll'** (a new kind of heavy beat jitterbugging) and heard **Helen Traubel**, (USA) the Wagnerian singer, defend her singing in night clubs because she could not sing the songs of 'Gershwin, Handy, Kern, Rodgers, Berlin and other great American composers' in the Metropolitan Opera House, this was also a time for dancing. Most of the bands played dance music, from **Bill Haley**'s Rock 'n Roll Group in the USA to **Johnny Dankworth**'s new band in Britain. One could dance, too, to special Coronation music such as *The Windsor Waltz, Coronation Rag* and *In a Golden Coach.* Highly popular in Britain and the USA for much of the time was *Eternally*, based on the theme song from the 1952 Chaplin film *Limelight.* Film music, indeed, dominated the popular market. A German song called *Answer me*, which began 'Answer me, Lord Above', was rejected by the BBC, but when the line was changed to 'Answer me, oh my love', nothing could stop it swiftly ascending to the top of the song charts, sung by **Frankie Laine** who at one time had three records in the top four.

Above: *Frankie Laine*

Below: *Benjamin Britten's* Gloriana *with Joan Cross as Elizabeth I*

The many emotive songs of the time included:

I talk to the trees
I've never been in love before
Don't let the stars get in your eyes
No other love
Little red monkey
Doggie in the window
Moulin Rouge theme

Perhaps the finest music to be heard by a massed audience in Britain was that rendered in Westminster Abbey during the Coronation service, the orchestra, organ, trumpeters and choirs producing sounds that stirred listeners to the roots. Beside this **Benjamin Britten's** opera *Gloriana* sounded a little thin, the best new music composed for the Coronation being **William Walton's** *Orb and Sceptre* and *Te Deum*. But of 1953's major works to survive on sheer merit, **Ralph Vaughan Williams's** *Sinfonia Antarctica* was to prove outstanding, based as it was on the music he had earlier written for the film *Scott of the Antarctic*, which admirably evoked the chill loneliness of that 'terrible place'. The operas of **Richard Strauss** were being performed to a much wider extent, including his later works, such as *Capriccio* by the Bavarian State Opera at Covent Garden. From the USA came distinctive contemporary sounds such as those in **William Schuman's** new baseball opera, *The Mighty Casey* and the *Concerto for Tap Dancer and Orchestra* played by **Morton Gould.** Of electronic music there appeared the first work issued commercially on a gramophone record, **Karlheinz Stockhausen's** (German) *Electronic Study I* and **the first studio for the production of electronic music** was set up in Milan.

Ballet and Ballroom Dancing

Ballet, like opera in Britain, paid its own tribute to Elizabeth II with a special production of **Frederick Ashton's** *Homage to the Queen* which **Sadler's Wells Ballet** took to the USA in its third tour of that country – an enormous success (like its predecessors) in a land where ballet was experiencing a sustained boom. Indeed there was a most healthy cross-fertilisation of ideas and styles throughout the ballet world with frequent overseas visits to many different countries by the various national companies. London, for example, saw **Ballets de Paris; Alicia Markova** of **Sadler's Wells** danced in Paris; **The New York City Ballet** toured Europe; and **the Royal Danish Ballet** played at Covent Garden.

Ballroom and Folk dancing, of course, absorbed the energies of the vast majority of serious dancers, the former well stimulated by **Victor Silvester** in Britain where formation dancing was becoming popular. As yet, however, such professional and amateur contests as took place were loosely organised, lacking an international set of rules.

Art

Pride of place in notoriety was taken by the competition sponsored by **an anonymous American** for a piece of sculpture on the subject of **'The Unknown Political Prisoner'.** Won by a Briton, the architect and blacksmith, **Reg Butler,** the model, a striking example of abstraction, was smashed while on display in the Tate Gallery by an outraged stateless Hungarian called **Laszlo Szilvassy,** but coolly reconstructed in a couple of days by its creator. Although the competition was largely ignored by the

Ballroom formation dancing

Above: *Reg Butler's controversial sculpture:* The Unknown Political Prisoner

Below: *Sir Gerald Kelly, president of the Royal Academy, discusses art with the moderns*

A fine example of early 50's commercial art

'recognised' sculptors, **Barbara Hepworth** was one who entered and took a prize. Strong disapproval was the reaction of the traditionalists but the ensuing debate was both stimulating and constructive. In New York, as it happened, an exhibition of **'Sculpture of the Twentieth Century'** was open-mindedly received though there was a rumpus over the display of **Renoir**'s nude bronze *Venus* outside the Portland Museum, Oregon. In London there were also a number of critical comments made about **Jacob Epstein's** *Virgin and Child* in the Convent of the Holy Child Jesus in Cavendish Square.

The Royal Academy at this time had a forthright and orthodox president, **Sir Gerald Kelly.** Several times he came into conflict with fellow artists and the general public. He objected, for example, to a sum of £30 000 being paid by the National Gallery for **Cezanne**'s *La Vieille au Chapelet*, **the top price of the year.** It is likely it would not have been realised at a public auction when art prices, in general, hung fire.

Literature and books

The high spot in literature was the award to **Sir Winston Churchill** (who became a Knight of the Garter in this year) of the **Nobel Prize for Literature** 'for his mastery in historical and biographical presentations and for his brilliant oratory in which he has stood forward as the defender of eternal human values'. In a year that was scarce of literary gems (excluding such works as **John Wheeler Bennett's** *Nemesis of Power*, **Cecil Woodham Smith**'s *The Reason Why* and **Alfred Duff Cooper**'s *'Old Men Forget'*) the greatest event may well have been the first ever public reading at Harvard University (in May) by Dylan Thomas – six months before his death – of his *Under Milk Wood*.

At 18 257, slightly fewer new titles were published in

Britain than in the previous year, though in the USA there was an increase to 11 255. *The Robe* by **Lloyd C Douglas** was acclaimed as the No. 1 Fiction seller in the USA while **Norman Vincent Peale**'s *The Power of Positive Thinking* came second only to The Bible in nonfiction. But a very dangerous move was made in the USA by the State Department, when it directed that books written by the supporters of Communism should be removed from overseas libraries. However, the President disapproved: 'Don't join the book-burners' he said. 'Don't be afraid to go to the library and read books' and the theme was taken up by those who watched the tide turning against the excessive bigotry of the anti-Communist groups. Public libraries everywhere found themselves in greater use. For example:

New York Circulating Library lent 10 335 810 books compared with 9 979 734 in 1952
The Public libraries of Paris lent 10% more than in 1952.
Britain's public libraries lent over 360 million books.

The increase in obscene publications was causing concern in Britain, however. Seizures by the police were up and in the Isle of Man a charge was brought against Boots Cash Chemists (who operated one of the largest and best known commercial lending libraries in Britain) for keeping an obscene book – two in fact – for hire. Judgment was given against Boots, though the Judge thought they had acted in good faith and that the books were no worse than those well-known by distinguished authors; a fine of £1 with costs was imposed.

Above: *Books for the inhabitants of rural areas*

Below: *A brilliant Welsh poet, Dylan Thomas, at the local*

SECTION 5

THE ARENA OF DISCOVERY AND PROGRESS

Constructional Engineering

The concentrated effort that went into improving and expanding so many inadequate roads and highways, prompted engineers to search for new methods that were both effective and economic. The most ambitious schemes emanated from the USA where the projected Tappan Zee bridge, to carry the New York State Thruway over the Hudson River, posed various problems which required novel if complex solutions.

● As **the world's heaviest cantilever bridge** (1212 ft (369 m) with 296 spans) it would require what turned out to be **the first example of floating box foundations.**

Times Square, New York, during a practice atomic air raid alert with the streets cleared of traffic and most people

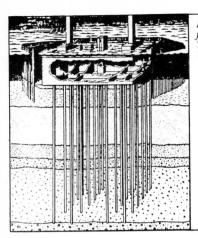

Plans for the floating box foundations and piles of the Tappan Zee Bridge, New York, USA

- A need for what were, then, **the longest steel piles driven** (only once surpassed since) at 270 ft (82 m).
- A demand for important changes in design caused by a complexity that raised costs well above the initial appropriation of $60 million. The original plan had to be modified by more than doubling the length of the main span and eliminating the primary concept of a tied-arch span.

Another type of project resulted from the discovery in 1951 that the famous **Golden Gate suspension bridge** at San Francisco oscillated through 85 in (215 cm) in a 72 mph (116 km/h) wind. This led to a commitment in 1953 to a $3.5 million scheme to stiffen the bridge and thus to improve its stability.

A world-wide shortage of steel, caused mainly by the rearmament programmes (and which had been felt in previous years), continued to encourage engineers to use more concrete than previously for all kinds of construction and to devise new methods. Over the Rhine at Worms was completed **the first ever concrete bridge,** weighing 5800 tons, across the navigable part of that river. The abutments of the structure which had been destroyed in 1945 were used and thus this pre-stressed concrete girder cantilever bridge included many features that were interesting, such as two hollow members and the joining of the cantilever arms by a shear pin.

Tunnelling methods were also undergoing fundamental changes through the much increased and improved use of rock bolts to support the tunnel roof in rock instead of by the traditional use of ribs and supports. The completion of the Woodhead Tunnel through the Pennines finalised work on what, at that moment, was **the longest railroad tunnel** (3 miles 66 yd (4.888 km)) **built in Britain in the 20th century.** Rates of advance were improved. Through rock at **Kemano** in Canada the tunnel went forward at an average 226 ft (69 m) per week spread over 12 weeks. Progress such as this encouraged those who dreamed of an **English Channel Tunnel** (upon the prospects of which there was fresh speculation that year), as a way of stimu-

The underground powerhouse excavated for the Kemano power project in Canada

lating continental trade. Throughout the world, however, numerous gigantic tunnelling projects were under consideration or nearing completion in connection with hydro-electric, road and railway schemes. In Japan, for example, **a 25 mile (40 km) railway tunnel was proposed between Honshu and Hokkaido** but would not be started until 1964, and 25 years later is still incomplete.

House building (see page 37) proceeded along traditional lines. But new methods in the use of machines were allied to the greater use of concrete which, in itself, hastened construction. Architects designed more imaginatively. Circular blocks of flats, a system long envisaged, sprang up in Sweden; buildings fabricated of concrete slabs and an accelerated movement towards more prefabrication were all to be seen – the latter in the shape of a new, experimental school at Wokingham in England with a steel frame and precast concrete-slab walls. Aluminium, too, was coming into more frequent use as, for example, on new hangars at London's growing Heath Row Airport and for the 8½ ton geodetic dome over the Ford Rotunda at Dearborn, USA.

Blocks of three and four storey flats in Stockholm. Each floor comprising ten one-room apartments placed in a fan-shape round a central staircase

Communications

Since telegraphs linked by cable were still the chief medium by which people 'spoke' directly to each other over long distances, the complete reconnection of **Cable and Wireless Ltd's North Atlantic cable,** cut in wartime in 1942, was of great importance, and all the more so since the modern cables employed doubled the line's original capacity. At the same time higher voice reproduction quality in land line communication was being introduced through **frequency modulated systems,** and in the USA **facsimile desk sets** (which would send and receive telegrams from one office to another in picture form) were being installed on a truly colossal scale (about 10 000 were in operation by the end of the year) by airlines, industry, news offices, and financial institutions – the Federal Reserve bank transferring over $1000 million a day by this method to other banks. This kind of system was

used to transmit, by radio, one 'still' Coronation picture every two minutes direct from Westminster Abbey to TV audiences in the USA, who were thus able to see the pictures seven minutes after the occurrence while listening to the sound broadcast direct.

A promising development, which has yet to be put to daily practical use, was announced: Bell Telephone's device called **Audrey** which could understand spoken numbers and translate them into telephone dialling instructions from 1 to 0. The USA was well in advance of other countries in its communications facilities; this year the 50 millionth telephone would be installed, nearly 80 per cent of them dial-operated, of which about 50 per cent were capable of dialling over long distances. In Europe nearly all such calls had still to be routed through operators.

Weather proof radio for American tractor drivers, kept farmers in constant touch with weather and market reports, sports events and entertainment

Wrist radio with a range of 40 miles developed for the US Army

The crucial matter of linking together the different countries of the world with better communications was advanced by the addition of the following line facilities.

Kuwait to Baghdad	telegraph
London to Jamaica	photo-telegraph
Athens to Rome	photo-telegraph
Tokyo to Hong Kong	photo-telegraph
Macao to the world network	telephone
New Caledonia to the world network	telephone
Syria to the world network	telephone
Turkey to the world network	telephone

Interesting patents applied for:
- **A gas turbine engine for motor cars** in the USA – some three years after an engine of similar category had started tests in Britain.
- **An ultrasonic fire and burglar alarm.**
- **A process for removing the cooked flavour from tinned milk.**
- **A method of giving meat a hickory smoke flavour.**
- **A way of taking the squeak out of shoes.**

Scientific and Medicinal Discoveries

Apart from the notable advances made in combating polio (see page 30), the battle against disease of every type was intensified. In August the *British Medical Journal* published information about **an artificial heart,** the result of work by **D G Melrose** and his team, that could be used to keep blood circulating during operations. But in those days, as now, mistakes could be made: **phenylbutazone,** while previously found to be useful in the control of arthritis, was also shown to produce many side-effects, some of which were dangerous if doses were excessive. Simi-

An artificial heart-lung machine in use in a Philadelphia hospital

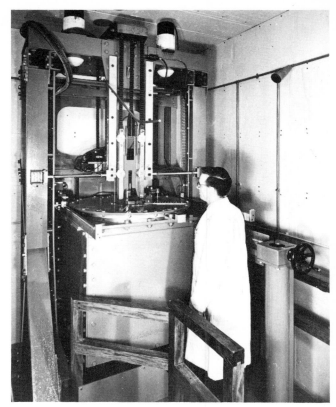

The fast breeder reactor at Harwell

larly the widespread use of the 'wonder' **antibiotic drugs** was already known to be building up high (sometimes 60 per cent) strains of resistance to their healing properties – a state of affairs that was almost beyond control in the USA where several drugs of this type were commercially available in quantity.

The dangers inherent in the construction of **'breeder' nuclear reactors** led to fears that an uncontrolled proliferation of nuclear waste materials produced by them would become a severe threat to public health. However, the breeder system had been proved feasible at Arco in the USA and there was a similar reactor being built at Harwell in Britain, projects which continue to the present day on a much larger scale. Everywhere, in fact, research on the most gigantic scale into atomics through synchrotrons, cyclotrons and all manner of accelerators and reactors went ahead with only the slightest public knowledge of what it all meant. Discoveries from research yielded real and beneficial achievements, and only rarely were failures publicised. For example, at the Harvard Hospital in Salisbury, Britain, attempts to find a cure for Influenza and the Common Cold, by means of a vaccine, produced only a marginal immunisation against influenza – and we are still plagued by colds 25 years later despite continuous research since 1953. On the other hand a scientific discovery, hardly commented upon at the time, was that of a catalyst derived from aluminium alkyl and titanium tetrachloride. It was discovered by a German chemist, **Karl Ziegler** (Nobel prize winner in 1963), and produced

Dr Alfred Kinsey (seated)

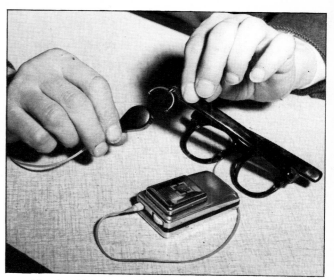

A hearing aid, its tiny conductor fits on the end of the spectacle frame; invented by Maurice Thomas, (British). Another good example of miniaturisation in electronics

an unexpected breakthrough which was to form the basis of nearly all subsequent man-made plastics, such as ethylene and butadienes (man-made rubber).

Perhaps the most sensational medical report of the year came under the title *Sexual Behavior in the Human Female* by **Alfred Kinsey** of the USA. Listed among the best sellers, mainly because of its startling behavioural revelations, this hefty statistical study was denied publicity by some 25 per cent of US newspapers on the grounds that it was not scientific, only sensational. Certainly some of its case histories seemed bizarre by the standards of the day, and informed judgment, 25 years later, while conceding that Kinsey made an honest attempt, throws doubt on his sampling procedures and his statistical analysis. Of far more solid and lasting value was the production in Britain by **James Watson** and **Francis Crick** of their celebrated mould which showed the structure of the DNA molecule and thus advanced the understanding of genes in heredity by a long way. Together with **Maurice Wilkins,** they were to receive the Nobel Prize in 1962 for their work.

Typical of the benefits which could be obtained from research and in which there was much activity in the laboratories were:

- **The new British white loaf,** claimed as the most nutritional yet made, which contained iron, vitamin B, and nicotinic acid.
- **Synthesis for the first time of the hormone from the master pituitary gland** with it associated insight into future studies of endocrinology.
- **Advances in the knowledge of steroids** along with the manufacture of **corticotropin,** the growth hormone. The development of anabolic steroids with their subsequent use by athletes and harmful side-effects, would follow later.
- The establishment at Nutfield in Britain of a **Brewing Industry Research Foundation** that was intended to be **the largest in the world** with aims of pure research that set it above the object of simply producing better beers.

Finally the most startling scientific exposure of the year was the demonstration that 1912's sensational discovery of an ancient skull, known as **Piltdown Man,** was a fraud. Modern chemical analysis by the British Museum, which housed the skull and had named it **Dawn Man,** proved that only the cranium bones were fossils; the other parts were from a modern ape disguised to look like fossils. At this time far more important and genuine discoveries of ancient skulls were being made in **South Africa,** one of which was 16 000 years old.

The phoney Piltdown Man skull

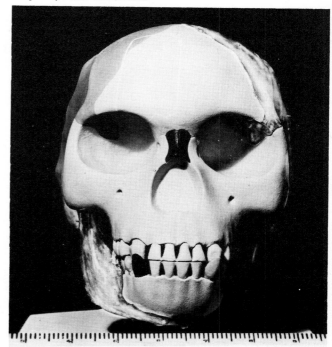

Discoveries in explorations

Archaelogically speaking this was a notable year packed with fabulous events. The announcement by **Michael Ventris** and **John Chadwick** (both British) that they had completed deciphering the famous **Linear B** Script, an exercise in statistical analysis, did more than prove that the inscriptions of certain tablets found in Greece and Crete were Greek (as hitherto was in doubt): it showed the way to a major change in the direction of classical studies. Linear B is the oldest known Greek script (developed by the Minoans and dating back to 1500 BC) and therefore a key to a reassessment of much work that had been done before, besides opening the door to a new view of ancient history. For this reason, the finding of more tablets in Linear B at **Mycenae** assumed an even greater importance now that they could be read. At Mycenae, too, a magnificent ivory group of goddesses was also found by Professor **A J Wace** (British) indicating the presence of a shrine.

Of the many places where fascinating discoveries of the past were being dug out of the ground, none were of greater importance than those in Palestine and Egypt. At Jericho **Dr Kathleen Kenyon's** epic scientific delvings were to do more than demolish claims, dating from the 1930s, that certain ruins were the celebrated biblical walls. No such walls had ever existed, she showed, but extensive Iron Age remains indicated that long before biblical times, in the 7th millennium, a community had lived on site protected by a massive wall. A valuable link was thus established with the earliest of civilisations. Likewise at **Saqqara,** near Cairo, **Dr Zakaria Goneim's** (German)

Examples of Linear B script from Knossos. Above: chariot tablet. Below: sword tablet

unearthing of a small pyramid, that was dated 6500 years of age, did more than establish the existence of **the oldest dressed-stone building in the world;** it acted as a starting point for an entirely fresh examination of the study of Egyptian history.

Other explorations of the Himalayan mountain range were overshadowed by the conquest of Everest (see page 18) but **Nanga Parbat** was climbed on 4 July by **Hermann Buhl,** a German, who did not use oxygen to reach its peak at 26 660 ft (8125 m).

Everest, half hidden by a shoulder of Chamlang (24 000 ft), seen from Nepal

Within the **Ruwenzori Range** of East Africa, an area that had been heavily reported upon in 1952, discoveries of four new mountain peaks and a glacier were made by the British ambassador to Ethiopia, **D Busk,** while he was on holiday there. Rather more deliberately, an expedition led by **Dr R Mairey** (French) set up **a new world record for cave exploration** by descending to a depth of 2395 ft (730 m) in the **Gouffre Lepineux** in the Pyrenees – that area of massive caves and underground waterways which had fascinated explorers for decades and, since 1953, has witnessed many additional record descents.

At **Young Sound, Greenland,** a British scientific expedition had made camp in July 1952 and continued to study meteorology and geology throughout the winter, supplied by air-drop and sledge parties. And in the **Falkland Islands** a British scientific survey proceeded to the accompaniment of complaints. Incursions were made by the Argentinians and Chileans (with claims on the islands), whose camps, erected without permission, were demolished by the British who deported the two occupants.

Beneath the ocean **Professor Auguste Piccard,** (Swiss) and his son **Jacques** on 30 September reached the greatest depth so far achieved by man (10 335 ft (3150 m)) in the Tyrrhenian Pit while encapsuled in the Italian bathyscaphe *Trieste*. Dramatic events such as this apart, those who spent much time under the water studying this virtually unknown region were coming up with a lot of new information about continental shelves, marine life and wave behaviour that would be of value in the future. With these things in mind, the scientists and politicians viewed with anxiety the mounting legislation by nations that attempted to extend their sovereignty in coastal regions beyond the 3 mile (4.8 km) limit (see page 44) in order to acquire valuable sources of food and minerals.

Above: *Five minute time exposure showing the eclipse of the Moon from Greenwich Observatory*

Dr Piccard starts deep dive from Trieste

The hunt for new mineral deposits was, of course, unending and the discovery of oil reserves in Western Australia was received with joy (unwarranted in the light of subsequent disappointing exploration) in much the same way as interested people in Southern Rhodesia and Tibet welcomed the unearthing of uranium in their lands. In Britain, where gas consumption was sharply up, a new programme (to cost £1 million over five years) of exploration for natural sources was begun with results that, 25 years later, have changed her prospects.

The expanding universe revealed still more secrets and suggested yet more intriguing possibilities as optical and radio telescopes probed its depths with mounting curiosity. Work started on the big steerable radio telescope at **Jodrell Bank,** England, and the Royal Observatory completed the first stage of its move from Greenwich to Herstmonceux Castle. The list of new stars, planets, comets, asteroids and galaxies was repeatedly extended as superior methods of detection and evaluation (such as the use of photo-electric cells and improved cameras) came into service. It was all very exciting though little understood by some brought up on a diet of science fiction and whose knowledge was only occasionally extended by an authoritative and lucid exposition on television by, for example, **Fred Hoyle.**

The explanation of wild life behaviour also owed much to the exposition of a scientist, **Konrad Lorenz,** whose *King Solomon's Ring,* published in 1952, came out in a Reprint Society edition. Among the important **wild life discoveries** was that **the bearded vulture,** for some time considered extinct in the Alps, was alive and domiciled in the Austrian Alps. There was an awakening sense of conservation in many places and a major effort in learning more by the British Severn Wildfowl Trust when it sent an expedition, under **Peter Scott,** to Iceland with the task of netting and ringing 9000 pink-footed geese prior to further study of this species and others. Migratory habits were under close examination so that a better understanding of bird life could be obtained everywhere in the struggle for their preservation as 'civilisation' threatened

their existence. On the other hand, **attacks by birds on civilisation,** were described in a report to the British Trust for Ornithology, which detailed the manner in which 'they', mainly tits, tore up wallpaper (which was top among their targets), newspapers, lampshades, public notices and all manner of clothing besides the fabric of buildings. Gipsy moth caterpillars also went on the rampage in New England, USA, consuming the foliage of 1.5 million trees. At about this time it was announced that some insects were developing resistance to DDT but that a new hydrocarbon insecticide, said to be non-poisonous to man and animals but 100 times more deadly than DDT, had been created. Public awareness of the danger of many insecticides was not then nearly so well informed, however, as it is 25 years later. There was an uncritical readiness on many people's part to accept, without some scepticism, the claims of scientists.

Peter Scott ringing pink-footed geese in Iceland

Prize Winners in Science

Nobel Prizes, each of which were valued at about £12 000, were awarded as follows:

The prize for **Physics** was won by **Fritz Zernike,** a Dutch physicist, whose outstanding contribution to optics and microscopy had brought about the introduction of phase-contrast microscopy, which made possible, without staining them, the study of living cells. As a professor in Gröningen University, he had been involved with astronomy, and it was his work on telescopic mirrors which led him to look closer at the phase-contrast method. In 1952 he had been awarded the Rumford Medal of the Royal Society.

The Chemistry prize went to a German, **Hermann Staudinger,** a biochemist in Freiburg University, for his work on plastics, particularly in connection with polymers – polymerisation being the process by which plastics, resins and rubber are synthesised and therefore of crucial im-

portance to industry (see also **Ziegler,** page 68).

The prize for **Medicine** was shared between two German biochemists who left Germany in the early 1930s and benefited from Rockefeller foundation fellowships in their complementary work. **Hans Krebs,** a refugee from the Nazis, worked at Cambridge University, England, moving in 1935 to Sheffield University. **Fritz Lipmann** began at the Rockefeller Institute, New York, in 1931, and then moved to Cornell Medical School. Krebs made what was called 'an historic contribution' by his discovery in 1937 of the citric-acid cycle (Krebs Cycle) in the metabolism of carbohydrates, the process by which cells burn and obtain energy from foodstuffs. Lipmann (with his associates) had, in 1947, managed the isolation of coenzyme A, a vital catalyst in cellular metabolism and thus closely related to Krebs' earlier achievements.

A real memory of the past was brought back when the 1953 **Daniel Guggenheim Aviation award** went to **Charles Lindbergh,** the first man to fly the Atlantic solo (in 1927), for 'pioneering achievement in flight and navigation'. Right up to the minute was the award of the **Harmon In-**

ternational Trophy to **Charles Yeager (USA)**, the first **person to fly faster than sound** (in 1947) and **Jacqueline Cochrane (USA)**, the **first woman to fly faster than sound** (652 mph (1049 km/h) on 18 May).

Other awards included:

- **The Priestly Medal,** the American Chemical Society's highest award, to **Sir Robert Robinson** (British).
- **Medals of the British Royal Society** to Sir Paul Fildes for research on bacteria and to Professor **Nevill Mott** for work on the Quantum Theory.
- **The Franklin Medal** of the Franklin Institute to **William Gibbs** (American).
- **Medal of the Royal Geographical Society** to **P T Baird** for exploration in the Canadian Arctic.
- **A very successful British claimant for monetary awards for wartime inventions** was **J Jablonsky,** who received a total of £17 000 for his work on aeroplane propellers and the Mosquito aircraft.

Above: *Nobel Prize-winner for physiology and medicine, Dr Fritz Lipmann with King Gustav of Sweden*

Nobel Prize-winner for medicine and physiology, Dr Hans Adolf Krebs

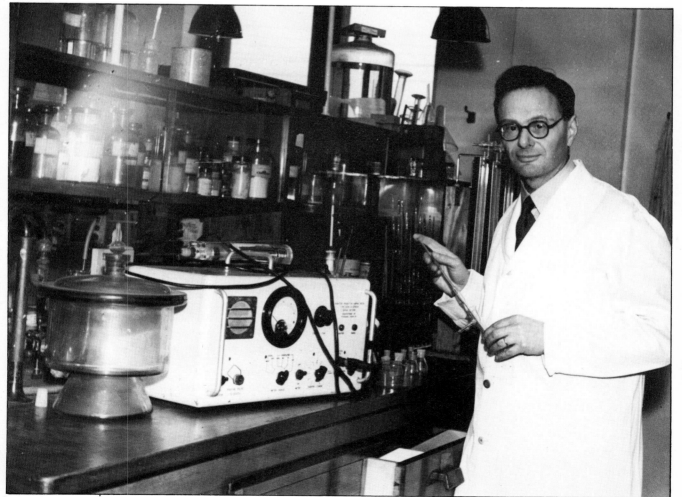

SECTION 6

SPORTS AND GAMES

The intensive study that was being directed into the playing of all manner of games, athletics high among them, was explained by **Roger Bannister** during a discussion at the British Association. As joint holder that year with **Chris Chataway, G W (Bill) Nankeville,** and **Don Seaman,** of the world record for the 4 × 1 mile relay (16 min 41 s) he claimed there was no limit to any physical performance but that it was psychological factors which reduced record breaking margins. Sheer force and mass of muscle counted for much and suitable training could develop it. Lack of oxygen limited improvements in long-distance events – as he himself was discovering, no doubt, while he prepared to run the mile faster than most people, achieving it this year in 4 min 2 s, just outside the world record. In fact, the year was to see no less than 37 world athletic records broken. But the existence of the element of chance in sports was exemplified in:

Angling

On 21 July when three beach anglers at Burton Bradstock in West Dorset caught ten bass with a combined weight of 104 lb (47 kg).

The world record holders of the 4 x 1 mile relay race at the White City: Chris Chataway, Don Seaman, Roger Bannister and Bill Nankeville

Athletics

No major championships were held in 1953, yet it was a year in which much progress was made. That remarkable athlete, **Emil Zatopek** (Czech), who the previous year had won three Olympic gold medals, again starred with new world records for 6 miles and 10 000 metres on 1 November at 29 min 8.4 s and 29 min 1.6 s, respectively. His 6 miles record improved on the 28 min 19.4 s effort by Britain's **Gordon Pirie,** then 22 years old, when he won the AAA title in July. At the even longer distance of the Marathon another great British athlete, **Jim Peters,** ran a magnificent series of races. He set a new world's best time of 2 h 18 min 34.8 s for the 26 miles 385 yards event.

Much attention was focused throughout the year on the Blue Riband event, the 1 mile, as the chase for the first sub 4 minute mile warmed up. The fastest time for eight years was set at 4 min 2 s by **Roger Bannister** (Britain) and **John Landy** (Australia) with **Wes Santee** (USA) clocking 4 min 2.4 s, although the latter was beaten by Pirie in the Emsley Carr mile. The barrier was to be broken in the next year. Another barrier under attack was the 7 ft high jump, and in winning his national title **Walt Davis** (USA) cleared 6 ft 11⅝ in to break the world record of 6 ft 11 in, which had stood since 1941. In the throwing events world records were set in all four men's events – **Parry O'Brien** (USA) 59 ft 2¼ in (18.04 m) Shot, **Fortune Gordien** (USA)

Mal Whitfield (USA), world record holder of the 880 yards and 1000 metres events, defeats Herb McKenley (Jamaica), World record holder at 440 yards, and Gene Cole (USA)

194 ft 6 in (59.28 m) Discus, **Sverre Strandli** (Norway) 204 ft 7 in (62.36 m) Hammer, and **'Bud' Held** (USA) 263 ft 10in (80.41 m) Javelin.

Fewer world records were set on the women's side, but notice of future intentions was served by the Soviet Union's women athletes. Soviet teams set three relay world records and individual record breakers were **Nina Otkalenko** at 800 metres – 2 min 7.3 s and **Galina Zybina** with 53 ft 1¾ in (16.20 m) in the Shot.

Jim Peters of the Essex Beagles, marathon runner, at Chiswick stadium.

Baseball

Any hope that **the World Series** might find a new winner was shattered when the **New York Yankees** defeated **Brooklyn Dodgers** by four games to two, thus becoming **the first club to win five times in succession.** Heroes of the series were **Carl Furillo** of Dodgers and **Billy Martin** of Yankees, the latter, 23 years later with team-mate **'Yoggi' Berra,** managing Yankees in a revival to reach the final after years in the wilderness.

Honours of the year went to:

Carl Furillo	Winner of the National League batting.
Roy Campanella (Dodgers)	Judged **most valuable player of the year** in the National League
Al Rosen (Cleveland)	Judged **most valuable player of the year** in the American League.
Carl Erskine (Dodgers)	**Record number of strike outs** (14) in third game of the World Series.

Legal event of the year. The Supreme Court, by 7–2, ruled that baseball was a sport, not a business.

Basketball

Inexorably the girls of **Baskin High School** went on to create an all-time record (begun in 1947) by winning 218 consecutive games, and the US ladies beat the girls of Chile by 49 to 36 in the **Women's World Championship.** As for the rest, 1952 NBA Champions, **Minneapolis,** repeated their win in the play-off over New York. The season's leading scorer was **Neil Johnston** of Philadelphia with 1564 points for an average of 22.3.

Billiards and Snooker

There was not much change among those at the top in these games. **Willie Mosconi** once more won the US pocket billiards championship (4th year running) and **Fred Davis** retained the British snooker championship against **Walter Donaldson.** Still supreme in snooker, however, was **Joe Davis** who scored his 500th century break on 18 February.

Ray Campanella of Brooklyn Dodgers and Billy Martin of the Yankees

Joe Davis – 500 century snooker breaks

Boxing

Supreme among the champions, each with more than one championship victory in the year, were:

Rocky Marciano, Heavy, who defeated

> **Jersey Joe Walcott** in May KO round 1
>
> **Roland La Starza** in September TKO round 1

Kid Gavilan, Welter, who defeated

> **Chuck Davey** in February TKO round 10
>
> **Carmen Basilio** in September on points
>
> **Johnny Bratton** in November on points

Jimmy Carter, Light, who defeated

> **Tommy Collins** in April TKO round 4
>
> **George Araujo** in June TKO round 13
>
> **Armand Savoie** in November KO round 5

And the winner of the Heavyweight bout of the US Golden Gloves Amateur contest was a man called **Charles (Sonny) Liston,** a future world champion.

As for British hopes of world honours, they were shattered when **Randolph Turpin** was beaten on points by **Carl (Bobo) Ohlson (USA)** for the Middleweight title.

Jimmy Carter floors Tommy Collins for the tenth time to score a knock-out in the 4th round of their lightweight world title fight

Cricket

Len Hutton puts one away watched by, right to left, *Arthur Morris and Lindsay Hassett*

Nothing else in sport seemed to matter more to many Englishmen than that Australia should be defeated in the Test Matches that summer in England. The Ashes had been held by Australia since 1934 and this year, with a very strong Australian team in prospect against a good England side, the chances of victory for England looked no better than evens. True, an inexperienced **South African** touring side had held the Australians to a tied series, two matches all in 1952/53, but the bowling of **Ray Lindwall** and **Keith Miller** looked as formidable as ever and **Neil Harvey** was in brilliant form with the bat. So **Lindsay Hassett**'s men were not really expected to relinquish the Ashes to **Len Hutton**'s team. The First Test at Nottingham set the tone; Australian batting displayed unexpected flaws, particularly against the pace bowling of **Alec Bedser** (who was to finish the series with a record total of 39 wickets). It was rain alone which deprived England of victory. The Second Test at Lords was memorable for **Len Hutton's last century for England** (145) against Australia, and a dogged rearguard of four hours at the end by **Trevor Bailey** (71) and **Willie Watson** (109) to stave off defeat. Rain again spoiled the drawn Third Test in which England were made to fight hard to save the follow-on, then to see Australia collapse to the spin of **Tony Lock** and **Jim Laker** and lose eight wickets for 35 runs. The Fourth Test was nearly Australia's; left to make 177 in two hours, through the aggressive batting of **Arthur Morris** and **Neil Harvey**, they nearly pulled it off. Amid terrific excitement the Fifth Test began at the Oval with England taking a first innings lead, thanks mainly to a fine innings of 82 by Hutton. But in the second innings Tony Lock took five for 45 and left England needing only 132 to win the series, a score they knocked off quite easily, after losing two wickets, mainly through the batting of **Denis Compton** and **Bill Edrich**.

Surrey won the County Championship for the second successive year, in what was to prove a string of seven successive wins, and **Len Hutton** had the best batting average (63.02) by an Englishman, although **Bill Johnston,** the Australian left-arm pace bowler, had a freak average of 102.00 with 16 not-outs in his 17 innings. For Oxford University a young batsman called **Colin Cowdrey** showed promise, topping the thousand runs for the season and scoring 116 against Cambridge.

Cycling

Italians dominated this sport with four world champions among whom **Fausto Coppi** was **the professional world champion** as well as winner in **the Tour of Italy. The Tour de France** was won by **Louis-Pierre Bobet** of France. Britons were also among the long-distance experts, **Ken Joy** capturing half the RRA records in one season, **Eileen Sheridan** (yet to reach the peak of her remarkable career) setting new records for Edinburgh to Glasgow and back (4 hr 26 min) and covering 250½ miles (403 km) in 12 h during her run from Edinburgh to London. However, it was **Edith Atkins** who took the most exacting women's honours by riding from Land's End to John O'Groats in 2 days 18 h 4 min, beating the professional record by some five hours.

Fencing

The names that had dominated the 1952 Olympics cropped up again in the World Championships at Brussels. **Christian d'Oriola** led France to victory in the foil team, as well as winning the individual title. **Pál Kovacs** (Hungary) won the sabre, as did his country as a team. And **Irene Camber** (Italy) once more took the women's foil event. **Italy,** indeed, were outstanding this year, winning all but the epée in the International Student Games at Dortmund.

Football (Association)

At Wembley a crowd of 100 000 paid a record sum of £49 900 to watch **Blackpool** beat **Bolton Wanderers** 4–3 in an FA Cup Final packed with drama. For one thing, this was seen as the last chance for the famous right winger, **Stanley Matthews,** to gain a cup-winner's medal. Bolton, however, scored in the first minute and were leading 3–2 15 min from time after a ding-dong struggle. By then they had two players injured (in days prior to substitutes being allowed), and the wizardry of Matthews was about to prove decisive. It was he who largely engineered the two goals which gave **Blackpool** the Cup in the closing minutes (making this the Matthews Final), though **Stanley Mortenson** had scored three of his team's four goals. In Scotland, **Rangers** won the cup, beating **Aberdeen** 1–0. **Pegasus** won the FA Amateur Cup for the second time in the five year's life of this club, beating **Harwich and Parkstone** 6–0 in the final.

Blackpool's captain, Johnson, chaired along with Stanley Matthews (right) *after winning the FA Cup*

For **England,** however, it was a traumatic year. Not only did they have to share the Home International Championship with Scotland, to whom they lost 2–1 at Wembley, but in November they forfeited their proud record of remaining undefeated by foreign nations at home. The match which went into history was at

Billy Wright of England exchanges pennants with Ferenc Puskas of Hungary before the match won by Hungary 6–3

The League winners in Britain were:

English League Division I		**Arsenal** beat **Preston North End** on goal average by .099 of a goal	54 pts
	Division II	**Sheffield United**	60 pts
	Division III (North)	**Oldham Athletic**	59 pts
	Division III (South)	**Bristol Rovers**	64 pts
Scottish League Division A		**Glasgow Rangers**	43 pts
	Division B	**Stirling Albion**	44 pts

Wembley in November, when England lost 6–3 to Hungary. The marvellous Hungarian team were to be acclaimed as the finest post-war side. Their great stars included Inside-Forwards **Ferenc Puskas** (their Captain) with **Sandor Kocsis**, Right-Half **Jozsef Bozsik** and Centre-Forward **Sandor Hidegkuti**. It was small consolation for England that, in front of a small crowd in the Yankee Stadium, New York, they were able, under floodlights, to beat the **USA** 6–3.

Rugby Union

England, undefeated, won the International Table by one point from **Wales** whom they beat 8–6 but on a day when the great **Cliff Morgan** was out of action due to injuries. Rather more remarkably, the **Australians** managed to defeat the **South Africans** by 18–14 (the latter's first international defeat since the war) but went on to lose the remaining four games of their tour by wide margins.

Wales versus France at Rugby in Paris

Rugby League

With crowds in decline due to disenchantment at play of unchecked violence, the paladins of Rugby League must have looked back on 1953 as a year to forget. A visiting **Australian** team did well in club matches, but was soundly beaten in each of the three Tests. **Huddersfield,** unexpectedly, won the Cup Final at Wembley 15–10, against St Helens, the Northern League Champions.

American Football (Grid-iron)

Voted Coach of the Year was **James Tatum** of the University of Maryland.

By 17–16 **Detroit Lions** for the second year in succession beat **Cleveland** in the play-off for the Professional Football Championship.

Ben Hogan, favourite for the Open golf championship.

Golf

Rated the greatest golfer of his day, **Ben Hogan** (USA) proceeded to justify that reputation by winning the US Open Championship (4th time), the British Open (1st time) and the US Masters (2nd time). US golfers (encouraged no doubt by that keen player President Eisenhower) dominated the world game but came very close to losing the Ryder Cup to Britain at Wentworth when they won by only 6½–5½, the tournament going to the last green where the British pair had only to get down in two 5s for victory and proceeded to take 6s! The USA also won the Walker Cup by nine matches to three.

Horse Racing

There can scarcely have been anybody in Britain (with the possible exception of bookmakers) who did not fervently wish, this Coronation Year, that the virtually permanently reigning champion jockey, **Sir Gordon Richards,**

should at last win a Derby; so far he had tried and failed 27 times. Six days after being knighted by the Queen, an enthusiastic supporter of racing, he mounted **Sir Victor Sassoon**'s **Pinza** to try again. Pinza, as it happened, was a great horse, and Richards brought him home to win by four lengths from the Queen's colt **Aureole.** Richards was again champion jockey (for the 26th and last time) with 191 winners, and Pinza consolidated his reputation as Horse of the Year by winning the King George VI and Queen Elizabeth stakes at Ascot, but just before the St Leger he strained a tendon and was retired to stud.

In the USA two horses, **Tom Fool** and **Native Dancer,** dominated; the former by winning all ten of his races, and taking home $256 355, the latter by winning nine races, including the Belmont Stakes, and achieving record winnings at $743 920. Native Dancer came second in the **Kentucky Derby** to **Dark Star.** The now fabulous **Willie Shoemaker** became the leading American jockey for the second time, but on this occasion with an astonishingly high record total of 485 in the season, 95 more than **Tony DeSprito**'s 390 the previous year.

Over the sticks in Britain the Grand National at Aintree was won by **Early Mist,** ridden by **Brian Marshall,** and the Cheltenham Gold Cup by **Knock Hard,** ridden by **Tim Molony** who was succeeded as National Hunt Champion Jockey by **Fred Winter,** with 121 wins.

Ice Skating and Ice Hockey

On 24 January **Rimma Zhukova** (USSR) skated 5000 metres at Medee, USSR, in 9 min 1.6 s to take the women's world record at this distance. She also won the 500 and 3000 metres at the Women's World Championships at Lillehammer, Norway, though the overall championship went to **Khalida Schegoleyeva,** also of the USSR. A Russian won the Men's World Championship, too – **Oleg**

Rimma Zhukova, Russian speed skater, after setting up two new world speed records over 3000 and 5000 m

Sir Gordon Richards achieved his life-long ambition by winning his first every Derby on 'Pinza'

Goncharenko who also won the 5000 and 10 000 metres individual events.

At Zürich the World and European ice hockey championships, thinly contested by only four senior teams, went to **Sweden.** Once more, in North America, **Detroit Redwings** won the National Hockey League but went down to **Boston Bruins** in the Stanley Cup who in turn were beaten by **Montreal Canadians** in the final series. To **Gordie Howe,** for the third successive season, went the Ross Trophy as top scorer (95 pts) and, for the second season, the Hart Trophy as Most Valuable Player.

Rowing

The tight finish of 1952 in the English Boat Race was not repeated this year. **Cambridge,** against the opinions of the pundits, came home winners by eight lengths in a race in which they were hardly headed. There was a somewhat tighter finish when **Harvard** beat **Yale,** though even here the difference between the two crews was 11 secs. Quite a few records were broken at Henley, but for the most part this was a year in which no one sculler or country dominated, each of the major events at the European Championships going to different men or nations, and no one club or person excelling in the sport in the USA either.

Swimming

Although the **Cross English Channel race,** sponsored by **Billy Butlin** for a prize of £500 for each winning man and woman, came to nothing since none of the seven competitors completed the course, the year was made remarkable by **Florence Chadwick** (USA) who, on 4 September, crossed the Channel in a much improved record time of 14 h 42 min (though she failed in an attempt on the

American swimmer Florence Chadwick during her successful crossing of the Bosporus, from Europe to Asia and back

double crossing). She also set a new record for crossing the Straits of Gibraltar (8 miles (12.8 km)) in 5 h 6 min, swam the Hellespont both ways (1½ miles (2.4 km)) in 1 h 58 min 8 s and the Bosporus both ways (3 miles (4.8 km)) in 1 h 14 min 7 s – all these endeavours being undertaken between 4 September and 9 October.

In a year that was deficient of great international championships there were, nevertheless, world record times in no less than 12 different events, four of them going to the USA, two each to Denmark, Hungary and the USSR.

Lawn Tennis

Youth out-shone all in the year that belonged to the 18-year-old **Maureen Connolly** (USA), who became **the first woman to achieve the Grand Slam** by winning the British, US, French and Australian championships, beating a string of distinguished players in the process. Another 18-year-old, **Ken Rosewall,** also upset the seedings by winning the Australian and French championships, but going out to the unseeded Dane, **Kurt Nielsen,** at Wimbledon and departing in the semi-finals of the US tournament to the eventual winner, **Tony Trabert.** Australian men's tennis was rising to a peak of accomplishment, however, **Lew Hoad, Ken Rosewall, Mervyn Rose** and **Rex Hartwig,** for the fourth time, bringing home the Davis Cup – but only by a narrow margin in the last match when Rosewall beat **Vic Seixas** 3 sets to 1.

Table Tennis

For the first time ever Britain won the Swaythling Cup, defeating Hungary by five games to three in Bucharest – though it has to be pointed out that England were advised by the great **Viktor Barna,** who had been in seven winning Hungarian teams before the war, and one of their team of five, **Richard Bergmann,** had played for Austria. Meanwhile a Hungarian, **Ferenc Sido,** was winner in all three mens events of the World Championships, as was the brilliant **Angelica Rozeanu** (Romania) among the women. **The Rumanian women** also managed to recover the Corbillon Cup from Britain.

Yachting

Ann Davison became **the first woman to sail across the Atlantic single-handed** when she arrived in the 4 ton *Felicity Ann* at Miami on 13 August, having taken 454 days, including generous stops at such watering places as the Azores en route.

A gathering of 31 vessels from seven countries that were swifter of passage assembled for the Fastnet Race in Britain, the American contingent of three being strong with boats each of which had won the Newport Bermuda event previously. But a British yacht (Class III), **Sir Michael Newton**'s *Favena,* won and British yachts were also second and third. The Americans had their revenge at Cowes where *Carina* (**R Nye**), won the Britannia Cup. On another occasion, too, a British 6 metre team, visiting the USA to compete in the British American Cup, was defeated at every appearance and lost by 29 to 39¼ points.

'Little Mo' Connolly (USA) in play with Ken Rosewall (Australia) at Wimbledon

SECTION 7

FASHION AND DRESS

A fall in the cost of raw materials used in the garment industry led to a reduction in the price of cloths, stimulating sales – particularly in export markets. This led in Britain to a production rise of some nine per cent, which brought the manufacturing side of the industry nearly to peak output.

Purchases of British clothes by the USA rose above the 1952 level by about 20 per cent – representing a total value of some £4 million – even though total retail sales of clothing fell in comparison with the previous year.

Nylon stockings – a much prized commodity of the times – were at last becoming more easily obtainable in Europe. Once exclusively produced in the United States,

Terry Thomas judges Southport beauty contestants wearing everyday summer dress

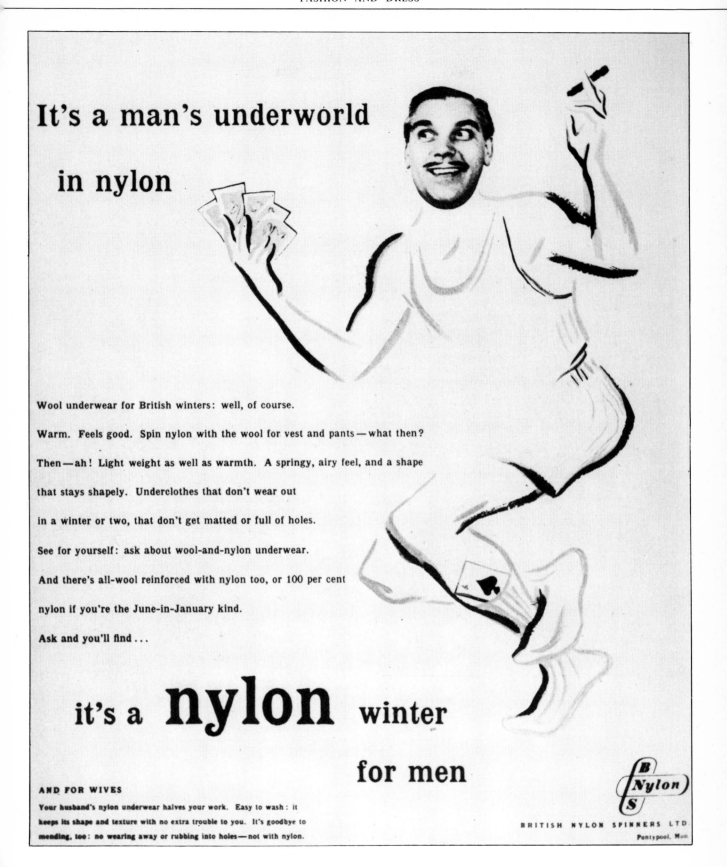

It's a man's underworld in nylon

Wool underwear for British winters: well, of course.

Warm. Feels good. Spin nylon with the wool for vest and pants—what then?

Then—ah! Light weight as well as warmth. A springy, airy feel, and a shape

that stays shapely. Underclothes that don't wear out

in a winter or two, that don't get matted or full of holes.

See for yourself: ask about wool-and-nylon underwear.

And there's all-wool reinforced with nylon too, or 100 per cent

nylon if you're the June-in-January kind.

Ask and you'll find . . .

it's a nylon winter for men

AND FOR WIVES
Your husband's nylon underwear halves your work. Easy to wash: it keeps its shape and texture with no extra trouble to you. It's goodbye to mending, too: no wearing away or rubbing into holes—not with nylon.

BRITISH NYLON SPINNERS LTD
Pontypool, Mon

they were now being manufactured, along with other nylon articles, in many other countries – to the detriment of US hosiery exports, which suffered a drop of 11 per cent compared with 1952. In Britain – unlike the USA – 'nylons' were still comparatively expensive, retailing at a cost of 6s 6d (32½p) a pair, but at least quality was improving: 82 per cent of nylon hose manufactured in 1953 was of 15 denier.

A feature of the world's textile manufacturing industry at the time was its adoption of increasingly sophisticated machinery, much of it designed in Britain. A number of new processes for blending man-made with natural fibres were under development; meanwhile drying, spinning and weaving machines were continually being converted from semi to fully automatic operation. **Carding,** for example, was being investigated by an electric analogue with the levelness of slubbing displayed on a screen.

It was, however, the increasing availability of **new synthetic fabrics,** including water-resistant rayons, which had the greatest impact on the clothing scene in 1953. Among these, the new British man-made polyester fibre, **Terylene,** which had been developed by ICI and put into production on a pilot plant, was showing particular promise. Confidence in the future success of this product led to a decision to double full-scale manufacturing capacity, scheduled to start in two years' time, and to produce it in France, Italy and West Germany. Thus the entire fashion industry found itself on the verge of a revolution, brought about by the wide range of new materials now at its disposal. The only problem was the slowness with which the new fibres were reaching the home market in any quantity.

For **women,** however, *haute couture* was not yet deeply committed to the new materials. For the most part the great Houses of Paris, London and New York continued to use the traditional wool, linen, silk and cotton, but these were now supplemented by rayon, and 'backed' or 'stiffened' by other synthetic materials. For example a new style of 'arched' skirt depended upon a material called **perlon,** the German equivalent of nylon.

In Paris, attention at the August collections concentrated on skirts, the length of which had been reduced by **Christian Dior** from 11 to 13 in (279–330 mm) to a daring 16 in (406 mm) from the ground. The same designer who had introduced very long skirts in 1947 with his famous New Look, Dior now sought to design skirts with a length more suited to the pace of modern life. With the active, younger woman in mind he wanted his clothes to reflect 'an eruption of youth'.

Fashion writers, perhaps trying to compensate for the dullness of the previous year, proclaimed that style was returning to the Twenties and the era of the Flapper. At least, however, there was now a theme to be detected, unlike 1952 which, apart from being the year of the 'wandering waist-line', was one in which no particular trend was discernible.

But the fashion houses did not influence sales universally nor did tailor-made clothing predominate. Even in France, 75 per cent of all women's clothing was bought ready to wear, and in other countries the proportion was much higher. The demand for crease-resistant or permanently pleated clothes, as yet only muted, was soon to deafen the market. Those who made and marketed shrink-resistant rayons were able to foretell this trend

Top model Barbara Goalen, the centrepiece for a collection of Coronation evening gowns

from the rate at which sales of clothing made from such materials were rising.

Bright and contrasting colours, together with imaginative pattern designs, characterised the clothes of the day. Blouses and dresses embellished with animal pictures or with animal-pelt effects were particularly popular. And, especially throughout the British Commonwealth, the Coronation theme of coronets and red velvet was reflected in clothing design and materials.

For the Street Parties young women turned out in long gowns, and thus were at variance with an increasing number who were beginning to prefer short dresses for evening wear.

Christian Dior's new shorter hemline – a daring 16 inches (40 cm) from the ground

The shop assistant in this outsize sale was kept busy removing and replacing the goods as they were sold

Joy Garraway in her Teddy Tinling nylon velvet swim suit braves a cold day by the sea

Typical holiday clothes of the time

The classic sports blazer, for town and country wear. The pattern cost 1 s 4 d (7p)

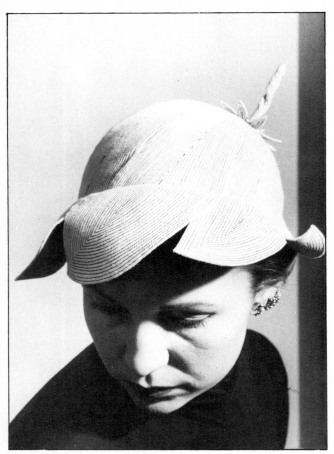

Above: *This snowdrop hat of white felt was worn with one of Digby Morton's new Spring Collection dresses*

Below:
From the leading London stores: shoes 49/9d (£2.49) Pearls 15/9d (£0.79) Gloves 14/11d (£0.74) Handbag 19/11d (£0.99) Chiffon scarf 3/– (£0.15p)

Although fur coats were not much in demand in the USA, it was there that most British-treated furs were sent, despite the fact that a mink coat made in London could cost £4500.

The absence of a clear change in trend in the design of foot wear (for example a preference for open sandals, similar in type to those seen in 1952, persisted) may have contributed in part to a slackening demand for leather, despite the fact that shoppers were buying more shoes than they had for many years. Since leather was already being replaced by the new synthetics as the principal material for shoes, the industry sought to improve its allure by promoting a National Leather Week in September.

Styles in jewellery followed a similar pattern to that in 1952; among precious stones, the emphasis was still on diamonds. For semi-precious stones there was a trend towards the use of modern settings. Still more artificial emeralds were available.

It was with the detail of their dress that men were concerned, though the fully draped Edwardian type of clothing continued in popularity even if it began to become associated – in some instances – with antisocial behaviour. The Norfolk jacket – with its pleats and outside pockets – worn with plus-four trousers, which had been re-introduced by the Duke of Edinburgh in 1952, thrived.

But for sheer splendour it was decorated waist-coats which took the eye. Fancy patterns were worn by leading show business personalities, among others, and even a Waistcoat Club was formed.

For evening wear, more ornate dinner jackets were now in vogue with a return in popularity of the single-breasted style – now sometimes seen in midnight blue – over the more traditional double-breasted kind in black. In line with this more colourful trend, full evening dress coats appeared with maroon silk linings to the tails.

But for everyday use men, like women, sought comfort in their clothes: turning more to shirts with integral soft collars in preference to the detachable type. This may have made dressing easier, but complicated laundering since, as yet, drip-dry, non-iron shirts were virtually unknown. Similarly, there was a trend towards self-supporting trousers and socks to the despair of brace and suspender manufacturers.

Generally, however, everyday clothing in 1953 was fairly conservative and only in those esoteric circles where *haute couture* dresses featured were there any marked changes to be observed. The clothes in the chain stores and boutiques were conversions from the previous year's high fashions into models that could be easily and reasonably cheaply mass-produced. Thus a wide range of prices covered seemingly identical articles, fundamental differences between which, however, were to be found in the quality of fabric used and in the standard of workmanship employed. People often complained that increasing mechanisation in manufacture was lowering standards but, 25 years later, there are probably as many who will assert that the clothes of 1953 were far better made than those of today.

The men's fancy waistcoat craze – long-lived by women's standards of changing fashion

The regular Saturday afternoon queue at a male hair styling salon in Hounslow

Prices in Britain were in the region of those shown in the table below:

What the smart interviewer and client wore

	£	s	d	
Women				
Brassière		16	11	(85p)
Pants		12	0	(60p)
One-piece dress	7	10	0	(£7.50)
Two-piece suit	20	0	0	
Coat	15	0	0	
Shoes	1	0	0	
Men				
Shirt (2 collars)	1	15	0	(£1.75)
Pants		5	0	(25p)
Three-piece suit	10	0	0	
Trousers	4	0	0	
Shoes	1	4	0	(£1.20)

Model of lady's costume and covering light-weight full length coat. Note the old 10/–note

SECTION 8

CRIME AND CALAMITIES

Salford traffic police were the first to wear an all-white uniform

Crime

Crimes of violence were dangerously on the increase in most countries of the world, a fact which had urgently to be taken into account by those involved in the shaping and administration of the criminal law. The knowledge that, in Britain, the rate of violent crime was three times above the 1939 level and that, in the USA, major crimes reached 2 159 080 (6 per cent higher than 1952), a figure which included 12 810 murders and 92 600 malicious woundings, led to insistent demands that something should be done. In Britain, where public attention was focused upon 'cosh attacks' by youths, **Sidney Silverman,** Labour MP for Nelson and Colne, tried unsuccessfully to introduce a motion in the House of Commons to reverse a decision by the Home Secretary, **Sir David Maxwell Fyfe,** to permit the hanging of a 19-year-old murderer, **Derek Bentley.** A few days later, on 13 February, a private member's bill, introduced by Wg Cdr **Eric Bullus,** Conservative MP for Wembley North, to restore birching as a penalty for people convicted of violent crime, was defeated at its second reading by 159 votes to 63. On 26 February, however, the **Prevention of Crime Bill** received an unopposed second reading, giving the police powers to deal with offenders in possession of proscribed offensive weapons, such as sand-filled socks, knuckle-dusters and sharpened articles.

London Police frisk a suspect in the street for concealed firearms

Theft, particularly of motor vehicles, was a growing problem in the USA, where 226 530 cars were stolen. Although 94 out of every 100 were recovered, the rate of successful prosecution in no way matched that figure. In cases of murder, however, the US police were fairly successful, making 94 arrests for every 100 killings, while 79 per cent of the 17 900 reported cases of rape resulted in a conviction. Nevertheless, it was a miracle, some thought, that crime was controlled as effectively as it was. Recruitment of police in Britain and many parts of Europe was especially difficult in the cities – where most crime took place. In the USA, and particularly in New York City, this problem was acute. There, a patrolman received $5000 per annum and would soon be on an eight hour, five day week, yet the entry qualifications had to be lowered at a time when the force stood in disrepute after 23 policemen (including five Captains) had been sacked for taking bribes from a bookmaker – a case in which nearly 200 others were also involved.

Among the more notorious crimes were:

● The celebrated affair of the house in Rillington Place, Notting Hill, London where **John Christie,** on his own admission, had strangled seven women (including his wife) since 1949 and concealed their remains, four bodies being found in this house. He was hanged on 15 July.
● The breaking of **a spy ring** in West Germany, allegedly run by Russian diplomats, and the arrest of 39 Germans, one of whom committed suicide. The ring was said to have been in existence for three years and to have been controlled in East Berlin, from the Institute of Economic and Scientific Research.
● The matter of **56 longshoremen of Jersey City,** USA, of whom in April, it was alleged by **Senator Charles Tobey,** that they were men with criminal records who had been given their jobs by a former mayor, **John Kenny.** In May the New York State Commission re-

John Christie of Rillington Place

commended that the Governor (**Tom Dewey**) be given authority to eliminate the links between local officials and organised crime, and that greater State control should be exercised over the waterfront (which was losing business) as well as the unions.

- The breakup of **an international drug smuggling ring in Marseilles** drew public attention to the vast traffic of this sort that was constantly in operation. Heroin came mainly from France, Turkey and Communist China; opium from Mexico, the Middle East and India with Communist China, having once been the principal supplier, declining rapidly as an exporter of this drug. In the USA the drug problem was serious, though the fact that 2500 oz (70 874 g) of opium seized in 1953 was less than the 11 800 oz (334 524 g) of 1952 indicated, perhaps, that shipments of the drug were, temporarily at least, on the wane.

- **The killing (with rat poison)** of housekeeper **Sarah Ricketts** at Blackpool, by **Louisa Merrifield** (46). She was charged jointly with the crime along with her husband, **Alfred Merrifield** (71) – though in his case the jury was unable to reach a decision and the charge was dropped. About Louisa Merrifield there was no doubt in the jury's mind; she was found guilty, her appeal was dismissed and she was hanged on 18 September.

The Merrifields of the Blackpool poison case. Alfred was released but Louisa found guilty and hanged.

The kidnappers of 6-year old Robert Greenlease chained and handcuffed leaving Kansas City Courthouse for the jail in which they were later executed

● **Two sensational burglaries:** that of the last jewellery of the **Hohenzollern family,** worth several million Marks, stolen from Burg Hohenzollern in Germany, and the theft of gems valued at £600 000 from **Seville cathedral** by a Spaniard of 19. The Hohenzollern case remained unsolved at the end of the year, but the Spaniard was arrested in London and all the Seville jewellery recovered.

● **The attacks by 250 armed civilians** on army posts in Cuba on 7 July that was repelled with the loss of 80 lives, subsequently represented by **President Fulgencio Batista** as part of a plot to assassinate him in a public uprising.

● **The Kidnapping of Robert Greenlease** (6) from school. A ransom of $600 000 was demanded and paid on 4 October for the return of this son of a wealthy Kansas, USA, car dealer. Three days later, however, **Carl Hall** was arrested with, it was said, $300 000 in his room and the boy's body then discovered buried in the back yard of **Bonnie Heady**'s house. On 18 December these two were executed in the gas chamber, she being **the first woman to be executed for kidnapping.** In the meantime, two police officers were sentenced to prison for perjury in connection with Hall's arrest, he having claimed that $590 000 was in his possession on arrest, a lot more than the $300 000 declared by the two policemen.

● **The bizarre sequel to the killing of Sir Jack Drummond and his wife,** while they were camping in France in 1952. More than a year after the crime, the two sons of **Gaston Dominici** accused their father (who had been on a holding charge) of its commission. After a further 24 hours' interrogation the father confessed and later attempted suicide. At the end of the year investigations were still going on.

Gaston Dominici, 77 year-old French farmer from Lurs, sentenced to death for the murder of the Drummond family.

Calamities

The year was not without its share of disasters, some of which caused widespread harm to thousands. The serious floods in Europe are described on page 14, though there were larger losses of life elsewhere in the world. Yet the accumulated death roll from accidents in homes, at work, on the road and in the air amounted to a much greater total than the sensational events that hit the headlines. For example:

Refrigerator deaths: Within the space of two days in August, eleven American children were suffocated through being shut in refrigerators.

Road deaths for the year were:

Britain	5090
USA	38 300 – the highest recorded up until then.

The highest number of fatal casualties in a road accident occurred in a bus crash at **Sison** in the Philippines on 15 February, when fire gutted the wreckage and killed 40 passengers. Another serious crash involving a bus travelling at night happened between Montreal and Toronto on 31 July, when a delivery van was hit by a bus which plunged 50 ft (15 m) into a canal at **Morrisburg,** Ontario. Many of the 37 on board were asleep and so were slow to react; 20 were drowned.

Air crash deaths: Excluding undeclared crashes behind the Iron and Bamboo curtains, and aircraft destroyed in combat in the various war zones, a count of announced air disasters reveals that 1373 died as the result of crashes. Of these the following were particularly distressing in view of the number of lives lost:

● 17 June at **São Paulo,** Brazil, when a *Constellation* airliner exploded, killing 56 people.

Twenty eight people were injured, but miraculously nobody was killed when this bus crashed over a parapet at Weehawken, New Jersey, USA

● 18 June at **Tachikawa Airfield** outside Tokyo, when two of the four engines of a US Air Force *C-124 Globemaster* failed on take-off in conditions of low visibility when cloud was down to 1000 ft (305 m). Trying to land, the aircraft fell short of the runway and caught fire, 129 men being killed in what, at that time, was **the worst air death toll in history.**

● 11 July at **Wake Island** when a *DC 6* airliner crashed, killing all 58 persons on board.

Since so many highly distinguished people travel by air it was inevitable that several should be lost in this way.

For example, air crashes were to claim the lives of **President Adolfo Cortines** of Mexico, **Jacques Thibaud,** the famous French violinist, and **William Kapell,** the American pianist.

The year's disasters were heralded on 1 January by a loud bang (**the worst industrial explosion of the year**) in a warehouse at **Valparaiso,** Chile which caused the deaths of 57 and injured 350. This was followed by **one of the most spectacular fires** of the year which began on 25 January in the liner *Empress of Canada* as she lay in Liverpool docks. Soon she was ablaze from bridge to stern and generating enormous heat that threatened dockside

The Empress of Canada, *burned out, lies on her side in Liverpool docks*

buildings. Two hundred firemen, plus river appliances, were called out to fight the outbreak, but they were beaten back by the flames. Holes were cut in the ship's side to gain access to the fire, but, with the volume of water being pumped aboard, she gradually took on a list and finally rolled over, her funnels crumpled and resting on the quay. Heavily booked to carry passengers from Canada to Britain for the Coronation, she was a total loss.

This was a bad year for ferries. When the 200 ton ferry boat *Chung Kyung* capsized in a hurricane at Pusan in South Korea on 9 January, 230 people were drowned, leaving only ten survivors. Among those who escaped was the captain, later to face charges of grave irresponsibility when it was found that the ferry had been overloaded. Only 17 days later another Korean ferry was to overturn, this time off Kunsan, with a loss of 113 out of 200 on board – and five days after that the British *Princess Victoria* went down in the Irish Sea (see page 15).

There were **four major earthquakes,** of which the shock that shattered **Turud,** Persia, on 12 February, was perhaps the most concentrated, though the one that occurred at **Chanak,** Turkey on 18 March was more widespread. The Turud'quake, which killed 531 people in an area of poor communication, happened in deep midwinter when the homeless were exposed to frightful privations and for whom help was difficult to deliver. That at **Chanak** killed 266 people, the shocks lasting most of the night and spreading as far as Istanbul, where there was panic in some cinemas. The third major earthquake occurred in three **Ionian Islands** on 9 August with shocks lasting intermittently until 3 September. Here four towns and several villages were virtually destroyed (25 000 houses completely) and 455 people were killed. By these standards the shock which caused severe damage in south-west **Cyprus** on 10 September may have seemed unimportant. Yet it was the worst in the island's history, making over 4000 homeless and killing 40. Terrible as the last disasters in and around Asia Minor were, they at least occurred in accessible places where rescue forces could be brought in by sea and air as well as along the land routes.

Scene of desolation at Waco, Texas, after twin tornadoes had struck the city

Of fires and explosions there were many of great if not ascending magnitude. A firework factory that blew up at **Fuchu** in Japan on 14 February killed 23 workers on the same day that a fire swept the waterfront of **Baltimore,** USA, laying waste to three factories and five piers at a cost estimated at $2 million. The loss of 33 lives in an old people's home at **Largo,** Florida, was caused by a blaze which began in the kitchen and swept through a dormitory at night. In terms of cost, however, **the most expensive conflagration of the year** was the one that devastated the General Motors transmission plant at Detroit on 13 August, killing two people and injuring 20, besides causing damage amounting to $50 million.

Several disasters at sea were the result of human error (see page 15), a trend that was re-emphasised by two naval catastrophes in the eastern Mediterranean area. Twelve miles (19 km) off Alexandria the Egyptian destroyer *Sollum* got into difficulties during a storm on 8 March, shipped water into her engine room and sent out a distress call which she later cancelled. Later still she called again saying she had broken down and was sinking. Nearby was a Polish ship, the *Czech,* which did its best in the darkness, though hampered by lack of a searchlight, to pick up the crew who had taken to liferafts. Fifty-three were lost, only 62 – including the captain – being saved. This turned out to be a bad year for the Egyptian navy when the frigate *Msir* was accidentally rammed and sunk on 16 May in the entrance to the Suez Canal. On 4 April the Swedish Merchant ship, *Naboland* under the command of **Oscar Lorentzon,** collided with the Turkish submarine *Dumlupinar* in the Sea of Marmara, sinking her with the loss of 81 men out of a crew of 86. Lorentzon was subsequently charged with negligence, found guilty and sentenced to six months imprisonment. Nobody knew, however, what had happened to the French ship *Monique* which had 120 people on board for a voyage to Australia, when it disappeared on or about 1 August, near New Caledonia. Almost as great a mystery were the explosions which damaged two aircraft carriers. On 3 February an explosion took place aboard HMS *Indomitable* while she was at **Malta,** killing seven sailors and injuring 30. And on 16 October, at **Boston,** Massachusetts, a far heavier explosion ripped through the USS *Leyte,* killing 37 and injuring 39.

On a much smaller scale was the loss on 8 February of the **Fraserburgh, Scotland,** lifeboat in heavy seas, just outside the harbour, with the drowning of six out of its complement of seven. Theirs were risks deliberately taken to help others, but the tragedy would lead in time to improvements in lifeboat design to make all lifeboats self-righting.

Railway accidents were fairly frequent occurrences, 29 Koreans dying in a derailment at **Iwon** on 3 January, and 21 Italians in a similar incident at **Benevento** on 15 February. A most spectacular crash occurred on 27 March at **Conneaut,** Ohio, after a piece of piping fell from a freight train, bent a rail and brought about the derailment of an 80 mph (129 km/h) passenger express, causing it to strike a passing freight train going in the opposite direction. Into the wreckage then ploughed another express, travelling at 80 mph (129 km/h). The collisions took place far from anywhere and one man had to run 3 miles (5 km) to raise the alarm. It seems to have been miraculous that only 21 died and that no more than 60

A tangle of smashed coaches litter the area after the crash at Conneaut, Ohio

were injured. Equally harrowing, was the crash that occurred when a London underground train ran into the back of another in a tunnel at Leytonstone, England. Twelve were killed and 40 injured, many of the victims being trapped in the wreckage for a long period. But for sheer horror and high casualties the worst rail accidents were reserved for the year's end (see page 111).

As usual many parts of the world were seriously damaged by storms, some of them almost as a matter of seasonal routine. The following list highlights the major disasters alone:

31 January	serious floods in **Britain** and the **Netherlands** (see page 14).
13 March	the first of many tornadoes hit the USA, bringing death and destruction **in Texas.**
11 May	more tornadoes in **Texas** killed 125 people and caused damage estimated at $50 million. In the wake of the torna-
	does came heavy rains and floods in south-west **Louisiana** (which had 12 in (305 mm) of rain in places) that created havoc, $200 million worth of damage and the deaths of 12 besides making 25 000 homeless.
22 May	tornadoes along the Canadian-US border killed ten people, bringing floods and extensive damage – particularly in **Ontario,** where the Riot Act was read in one place to prevent further looting of unoccupied property. Further tornadoes in **Ohio** and **Massachusetts** on 8 and 9 June killed 107 more, which did extensive damage estimated at well over $50 million. In at least one case early warning was sent to the threatened area by radio 'hams'.
25 June	heavy rains, stated as causing **the worst floods in modern history,** made 1 million people homeless on Kyushu Island, Japan and killed 684. In the middle of July came more heavy rain, this time on

A homeless family, carrying the few personal belongings they had managed to salvage, trudging almost knee-deep in water along a street in Konshu, Japan

Honshu, breaking three river banks, threatening **Tokyo** and killing 640 people. Then on 16 August, the **Taisho Dam** across the **Yodo River** in Honshu collapsed and killed a further 370 people. Still the tale of disaster in Japan was incomplete, for on 25 September a typhoon killed 125 in the south, the same day on which a different typhoon struck war-torn Vietnam and killed an estimated 1000 people.

1 August   **a heat wave** having caused 158 deaths in Southern Persia in mid-July, 'flash' floods at **Khurtrudbar** in the north drowned some 450 people, and another flash flood on the 4th at **Vaz** took a further 265.

Heavy rains were a feature of the year in so many places. Yet President Eisenhower at one time felt the need to ask for $150 million aid for parts of Texas, Oklahoma, Missouri and other south-western states to alleviate the effects of **a major drought** that had persisted from the previous year and had resulted in serious soil erosion.

15 October   heavy rains in the Mediterranean led to extensive flooding in a number of places. In **Northern Spain** 50 people lost their lives and damage was put at $20 million. In **Reggio Calabria,** Italy, a fortnight of almost ceaseless downpour produced widespread floods, some of the deadly 'flash' nature, which took a toll of 62 lives and caused much damage.

The number of big mine disasters was about average, beginning with the loss of 18 miners at **Chalus,** Persia, on 22 January, when a roof caved in. On 19 March 19 miners were killed on **Spitzbergen Island** in an underground explosion; on 27 September 12 died in a pit at **Quarernon,** Belgium, when a lift cage fell down its shaft and a few days later, again in Belgium but this time at **Seraing,** 30 miners were killed by an explosion.

The second most lethal single industrial explosion of the year, seems to have been that which occurred in an ammunition dump at **Nantsechu,** Formosa, where a large collection of old Japanese torpedoes detonated on 6 April, killing 50 people and injuring 250.

The most insidious outbreak of a killer disease may well have been the **gastroenteritis** that killed 58 children in **Priente Province, Cuba** during the summer, an epidemic believed to have been caused by the spread of equine encephalitis that had killed over 30 000 horses in six weeks.

Just when the vast majority of Christian families (and many others besides) were gathering on Christmas eve, **the final and most catastrophic of the year's railway accidents occurred.**

Near Sakvice in Czechoslovakia, the Bratislava to Prague express charged into the back of a local train, scattering wreckage, killing 103 people and injuring 83. A signalling error was thought to be the cause.

An even worse disaster took place that evening in New Zealand where water within the extinct volcanic crater of Mount Ruapeku (9000 ft (2743 m)) broke through the wall of a tunnel and poured out to collapse the bridge over the **River Wangachu, Tangiwai,** that carried the railway line from Auckland to Wellington. A moment later an express with 270 passengers was due to cross. In fact the local postmaster, **C Ellis,** had seen the bridge fall and tried hard to attract the locomotive driver's attention, but to no avail and Mr Ellis had to leap to safety. The train plunged into the torrent below and its carriages were smashed or swept away, one of them cut in two, another to be found later five miles downstream. One coach lay balanced on the brink with Mr Ellis desperately trying to arouse the dazed passengers to their peril; but the coupling snapped and the coach dropped into the water with the rest, leaving only three coaches and the guard's van out of harm's way. The final death roll was 146. This disaster was the subject for a sad note in the Queen's Christmas radio speech to the Commonwealth next day, from where she was staying in New Zealand at the time.

The rail crash at Tangiwai, New Zealand

SECTION 9
OBITUARIES

Among the distinguished people who died in 1953 were:

● **Hilaire Belloc** (b 1870), son of a French father and English mother, whose earlier reputation as an orator and Member of Parliament was later overshadowed by his talent for writing, whether of a journalistic, political, poetic or literary style and nature. Closely associated at one time with **G K Chesterton,** he was as at home in compiling biographies or commentaries on war as he was in writing poetry for children. For sheer versatility he was a giant, his books encompassing religious subjects, travel and a four volume history of England besides several satirical novels and a great many brilliant essays.

● **Lavrenti Beria** (b 1899), whose career in the Russian Communist Party began in 1917 and was spent for the most part in intelligence and counter-intelligence work that carried him, in 1938, to the command of the NKVD (People's Commissariat of Internal Affairs). As a close collaborator of **Josef Stalin** (see page 15) he was deeply involved in the imposition of the Russian dictatorship and the ruthless elimination of dissidents. As a deputy prime minister and member of the five man Defence Council, formed shortly after the German invasion in 1941, he was largely responsible for the organisation of arms production. After the war he joined the Politburo with the rank of Marshal of the Soviet Union and was

Josef Stalin lies in state in the House of the Unions, near the Kremlin

Kathleen Ferrier gives a Lieder recital with Bruno Walter at the piano at the Usher Hall, Edinburgh

again placed in overall command of Security in the Communist Police State. With the death of Stalin his fate was sealed . . . (see page 17).

● **Margaret Bondfield** (b 1873), who was the first British woman to acquire the rank of Cabinet Minister, holding the post of Minister of Labour in Ramsay MacDonald's Labour Government of 1929–31. First a shop assistant and subsequently a Trade Unionist, who became secretary of the National Federation of Women Workers in 1921, she was made Chairman of the Trades Union Congress of 1923 (the first woman to be so) and in that year was elected Member of Parliament. Defeated in the election of 1931, she did not again return to the centre of the political scene.

● **Carol II** (b 1893), ex-King of Romania, whose stormy political and domestic career several times hit the headlines. His association with **Helena Magda Lupescu** led to an enforced abdication in 1926 of his rights to the throne. Brought back to a regency in 1930, he managed to regain

the throne and keep Mme Lupescu at his side. His attempts to maintain a balance between rival political factions and retain the power of the throne while resisting external pressures from Germany, on the one hand, and Russia, on the other, could be little more than a dictatorial exercise in delay. In 1940 he was forced to cede Bessarabia to Russia and Transylvania to Hungary; in September of that year he was forced finally into exile.

● **Kathleen Ferrier** (b 1912), a former British telephone operator who, at the age of 28, had won a local singing competition as the outcome of a dare, and by 1946 was an established contralto of the first rank. Her voice continued to develop in quality and expression until her premature death from cancer, most courageously borne. She was adored by the public as well as by her friends for her charmingly high spirits and out-going personality. Her interpretation of the works of **Gustav Mahler** was supreme. There was something ethereal about her singing which made her incomparable as an artiste and as a star, whose rising was late and whose brilliance was so full of lustre that her sudden, rapid extinction at the zenith of her career came as a dreadful shock.

● **Klement Gottwald** (b 1896), Communist prime minister of Czechoslovakia (1846–8) under **Dr Edward Beneš** until the latter was forced to resign as President in 1948 when the Communists seized power. Quite as ruthless as Stalin, it was he as much as anybody else who destroyed the democratic system in his country and persecuted those in opposition to him. For the cause of his death see page 15.

● **Ibn Saud** (b 1880), King of Saudi Arabia and founder of that state in 1932 who, with 15 comrades, seized the capital of Arabia, Riyadh, in 1901, and from then on expanded his hold upon the country with a view to establishing a unified, independent nation, free from tribal turmoil, Turkish occupation and British influence. By calling upon the religious fervour of his Moslem followers, he achieved unity; by limited military operations prior to 1914, he began to eject the Turks and, with the help of the British, completed their removal during the First World War. Still with British assistance after the war he finalised the conquest of those territories which, 25 years later, largely make up Saudi Arabia. Ruthlessly he defeated the Arab princes who opposed him, and put down each revolt as it occurred. His main aim, however, was to achieve peace with his neighbours through diplomacy, and the creation of a modern state financed by oil revenues from a concession granted to the American oil company Aramco in 1933. In 1945 Saudi Arabia became a founder member of the Arab League and was later taken by Ibn Saud into the United Nations.

● **Mary** (b 1867), dowager Queen Mother of Britain and the widow of King George V, who occupied a position of particular affection in the minds of the British people over many years for her dignity, benevolence and compassion.

King Ibn Saud of Saudi Arabia

Queen Mary's official jubilee portrait taken in 1935

Tazio Nuvolari at the wheel of his Alfa Romeo

Virtually destined from birth to be a queen, she was originally engaged to the **Duke of Clarence,** eldest son of the Prince of Wales who, in 1901, was to become **Edward VII.** But in 1893, after Clarence's death, she married his younger brother and became Queen in 1910 when he succeded to the throne as **George V.** Among the tragedies in her life apart from Clarence's premature demise, was the death at the age of 16 of John, her youngest son, the abdication of her eldest son, **Edward VIII,** in 1936, the death on active service of another son, **the Duke of Kent** in 1943, and the death of **George VI** in 1952. By her death on 24 March she was denied a part in the Coronation of her grand-daughter.

● **Tazio Nuvolari** (b 1892), winner of the Italian Motor Cycling Grand Prix in 1925 and subsequently one of the most successful motor racing drivers, with more than 50 major victories to his credit and a skill which enabled him to defeat lesser drivers or cars of superior technical merit. Not for nothing was this 5 ft (1.52 m) tall Italian known as **Il Maestro** and rated the greatest racing driver of his era. Nor was he the 'property' of any one motor manufacturer, driving as he did Bianchis, Chiribiris, Bugattis, Alfa Romeos, Maseratis, MGs, Auto Unions, Cisitalias and Ferraris.

● **Sergei Prokofiev** (b 1891), Russian composer famous for his opera and ballet music, and beloved by children as well as adults for his orchestral suite with spoken accompaniment, **Peter and the Wolf.** A modernist and a brilliant pianist, he spent the last 20 years of his life in Russia (having previously lived much of his time in the West) where he somehow managed to bend his individualistic talent to accommodate the rigid demands of the political regime. Even so he clashed with the Soviet

authorities and was several times suppressed by censorship and criticism.

● **Josef Stalin** (b 1879), a Georgian shoemaker's son who, via insurrectionist activities (allied to bank robbery) and deportation to Siberia (from where he escaped in 1904), rose to be the first editor of *Pravda* (the Russian Communist Party's official newspaper) and by stages to a prominent position in the Bolshevik Government of **Lenin.** Though insignificant in the revolution itself, he became prominent in its aftermath and, by 1923, strong enough to prevent **Trotski** from succeeding Lenin upon the latter's death. In the years to come he so strengthened his position that he was virtual dictator,

Sergei Prokofiev

putting down all opposition by the most ruthless application of power, using terror, massed deportations and imprisonments as his weapons, killing those in authority who opposed him, and employing genocide to implement the land reforms and the collectivisation of the farms in the 1930s. Associated with these horrors was the large-scale rearmament which failed to save Russian forces from their initial disastrous defeats at German hands in 1941 and 1942, because he had killed so many of the best leaders. Stalin is best remembered for his command of the Soviet forces in defeating the German invasion, for his subsequent imposition of Soviet style rule upon the eastern European states that fell to the Red Army, and for his implacable determination to spread Soviet domination by all practical means at his disposal. Although after his death he was to be demoted in esteem by his successors, in life he was too formidable to be challenged.

● **Robert Taft** (b 1889), four times unsuccessful candidate for the Republican nomination for the US presidency and one of the most influential US politicians of his day. From leader of the Republican Party in the House of Representatives in 1925 he progressed well until rejected by the electorate of the party and by **President Roosevelt** and the Democrats in 1932. Returning as a Senator in 1938, he was a tough opponent of the New Deal in the days when it was failing in credibility under attack. Isolationist though he was, he supported the war effort after Pearl Harbor. Mainly, however, he was dedicated to domestic issues of a conservative nature, the restrictive Taft–Hartley Labor Management Relations Act of 1947 being fairly representative of his inclinations and work. Denied by Eisenhower the presidential nomination in 1952, he nevertheless gave unselfish support to his rival and, with the Republican victory, emerged as a dominant figure in the new Administration as Eisenhower's chief adviser in the Senate and already a strong influence to guide the ex-soldier. No sooner was his new political power developing, however, when cancer struck fast and hard and he died on 31 July after a short illness. In 1957 he was selected by Congress as one of five past Senators with outstanding abilities.

Robert Taft

Others of Distinction Who Died in 1953 Included

Ernest Barnes	b 1874	British	Bishop, mathematician and controversial preacher
Sir Arnold Bax	b 1883	British	Composer and Master of the King's Music since 1942
Sir Muirhead Bone	b 1876	British	Artist and engraver
Gordon Campbell VC	b 1886	British	Q Ship captain, one time MP
Fred Darling	b 1884	British	Race horse trainer with 7 Derbys to his credit
René Fonck	b 1894	French	First World War air 'ace' with 75 confirmed victories
Hunting Horse	b 1846	American	Indian scout for **General George Custer**
Alex James	b 1901	British	Scottish and Arsenal footballer
Cyril Joad	b 1891	British	Philosopher and broadcaster
Sir Edward Marsh	b 1872	British	Art collector, writer and civil servant
Shyama Mockerjee	b 1901	Indian	Lawyer and politician, Member of Congress
Eugene O'Neill	b 1888	American	Dramatist and Nobel Prize Winner for literature
Nikolaos Plastiras	b 1883	Greek	Soldier, radical politician and three times prime minister
Ernst Reuter	b 1889	German	Mayor of Berlin during the days of the air bridge
Gerd von Rundstedt	b 1875	German	Field-Marshal who commanded German army groups in the Second World War
Jacques Thibaud	b 1880	French	Violinist and teacher of music
Dylan Thomas	b 1914	British	Writer and poet
William Tilden	b 1893	American	Lawn Tennis player
Frederick Vinson	b 1890	American	Chief Justice of the USA
Jonathan Wainwright	b 1883	American	American General, defender of Bataan and Corregidor, 1941/2

Advertising

To those looking back over a period of time, it is perhaps true to say that nothing reflects the flavour of a year better than its advertising.

In the following pages three advertisements for well known products are shown. These products continue as leading brands today, but their advertising has changed considerably over the years. The style and format of the advertisements illustrated are typical of twenty five years ago.

Opening Time is Guinness Time

BREAD AND CHEESE and a Guinness is a meal in itself — just what you need to keep you going when you haven't time for a big meal. The clean invigorating taste of Guinness is splendidly welcome when you are tired at midday, or after work. And its goodness makes you feel you've really had something worth drinking.

GUINNESS

does **more**

than quench

your thirst

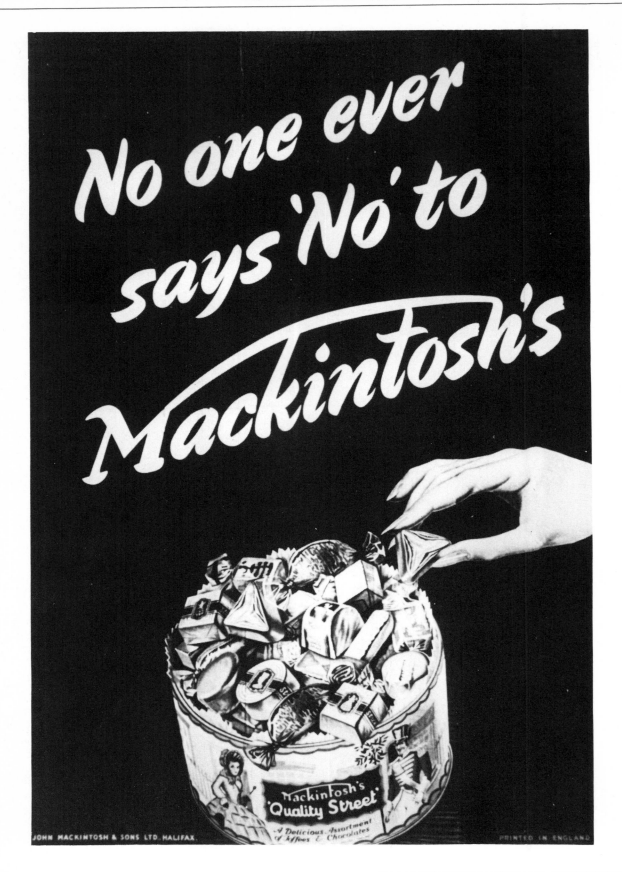

"Mummy says Hot OXO is a sure way to melt a man's heart."

FOR NOURISHMENT AND FLAVOUR

ENJOY THE STIMULATING PROPERTIES OF PRIME BEEF

OTHER GUINNESS SUPERLATIVES TITLES

Facts and Feats Series:

Air Facts and Feats, *3rd ed.*
John W. R. Taylor, Michael
J. H. Taylor and David Mondey

Rail Facts and Feats, *2nd ed.*
John Marshall

Tank Facts and Feats, *2nd ed.*
Kenneth Macksey

Yachting Facts and Feats
Peter Johnson

Plant Facts and Feats
William G. Duncalf

**Structures—Bridges, Towers,
Tunnels, Dams . . .**
John H. Stephens

Car Facts and Feats, *2nd ed.*
edited by Anthony Harding

Business World
Henry Button and Andrew Lampert

Music Facts and Feats
Bob and Celia Dearling

Animal Facts and Feats, *2nd ed.*
Gerald L. Wood

Weather Facts and Feats
Ingrid Holford

Astronomy Facts and Feats
Patrick Moore

Art Facts and Feats
John FitzMaurice Mills

Guide Series:

Guide to Saltwater Angling
Brian Harris

Guide to Freshwater Animals
Brian Harris and Paul Boyer

Guide to Mountain Animals
R. P. Bille

Guide to Underwater Life
C. Petron and J. B. Lozet

Guide to Motorcycling, *2nd ed.*
Christian Lacombe

**Guide to French
Country Cooking**
Christian Roland Délu

Guide to Bicycling
Jean Durry and J. B. Wadley

Guide to Water Skiing
David Nations OBE and
Kevin Desmond

Other titles:

**The Guinness Guide to Feminine
Achievements**
Joan and Kenneth Macksey

The Guinness Book of Names
Leslie Dunkling

Battle Dress
Frederick Wilkinson

Universal Soldier
edited by Martin Windrow and
Frederick Wilkinson

History of Land Warfare
Kenneth Macksey

History of Sea Warfare
Lt.-Cmdr. Gervis Frere-Cook and
Kenneth Macksey

History of Air Warfare
David Brown, Christopher Shores
and Kenneth Macksey

The Guinness Book of Answers
edited by Norris D. McWhirter

The Guinness Book of Records,
edited by Norris D. McWhirter

The Guinness Book of 1952
Kenneth Macksey

100 Years of Wimbledon
Lance Tingay

British Hit Singles
Jo and Tim Rice

THE GUINNESS BOOK OF

1952

LAST TRAM WEEK
ON JULY 5 WE SAY GOODBYE TO LONDON

Kenneth Macksey